BRAZIL AT THE DAWN OF
THE EIGHTEENTH CENTURY

CULTURA,
E OPULENCIA
DO BRASIL

POR SUAS DROGAS, E MINAS,

Com varias noticias curiosas do modo de fazer o Assucar; plantar,
& beneficiar o Tabaco; tirar Ouro das Minas; & descu-
brir as da Prata;

*E dos grandes emolumentos, que esta Conquista da America Meridional
dá ao Reyno de PORTUGAL com estes, & outros gene-
ros, & Contratos Reaes.*

OBRA
DE ANDRE JOAO ANTONIL

OFFERECIDA

Aos que desejaõ ver glorificado nos Altares ao Veneravel Padre JOSEPH DE ANCHIETA
Sacerdote da Companhia de JESU, Missionario Apostolico, & novo Thau-
maturgo do Brasil.

SEMPER HONORE MEO

LISBOA,
Na Officina Real DESLANDESIANA.
Com as licenças necessarias Anno de 1711.

BRAZIL
at the Dawn of the
Eighteenth Century

André João Antonil

Translated and edited by Timothy J. Coates,
completing a partial translation begun
by Charles R. Boxer

Preface by Stuart B. Schwartz

Tagus Press | *UMass Dartmouth*
DARTMOUTH, MASSACHUSETTS

Classic Histories from the
Portuguese-Speaking World in Translation 1

Series Editors: Timothy J. Coates and Timothy D. Walker

Tagus Press at UMass Dartmouth
www.portstudies.umassd.edu

General Editor: Frank F. Sousa
Managing Editor: Mario Pereira
Copyedited by Martin Hanft
Designed by April Leidig
Typeset in Caslon by Copperline Book Services, Inc.

Tagus Press books are produced and distributed for Tagus Press by University
Press of New England, which is a member of the Green Press Initiative. The
paper used in this book meets their minimum requirement for recycled paper.

For all inquiries, please contact:
Tagus Press at UMass Dartmouth
Center for Portuguese Studies and Culture
285 Old Westport Road
North Dartmouth MA 02747-2300
Tel. 508-999-8255
Fax 508-999-9272
www.portstudies.umassd.edu

Partial translation of Cultura e Opulência do Brasil begun by Charles R. Boxer
used courtesy Lilly Library, Indiana University, Bloomington, Indiana; and
Carola Vecchio and the estate of Charles R. Boxer.

MINISTÉRIO DA CULTURA
Fundação BIBLIOTECA NACIONAL

This work was published with the support of the
Brazilian Ministry of Culture/National Library Foundation.
Obra publicada com o apoio do Ministério da Cultura do
Brasil/Fundação Biblioteca Nacional.

5 4 3 2 1

FRONTIS: Title page from André João Antonil, *Cultura e Opulência do Brasil*,
Lisbon, 1711; original edition at John Carter Brown Library, Providence, Rhode
Island. Courtesy of the John Carter Brown Library at Brown University.

CONTENTS

Preface by Stuart B. Schwartz xi

Introduction xv

BRAZIL AT THE DAWN OF
THE EIGHTEENTH CENTURY I

THE FIRST PART
*The Agricultural Wealth of Brazil in the
Cultivation of Sugar* 7

Preamble 9

BOOK I

CHAPTER I: The Resources a Royal Sugar
Mill Owner Should Possess 15

CHAPTER II: How the Sugar Planter Should Act in
the Purchase, Upkeep, and Leasing of His Lands 19

CHAPTER III: How the Planter Should Deal with Tenants
and His Other Neighbors and They with Him 22

CHAPTER IV: How the Planter Should Behave in Choosing
the Hands and Skilled Workers He Engages, Beginning
with the Choice of Chaplain 25

CHAPTER V: The Head Overseer and the Subordinate
Overseers Who Preside in the Milling, the Estate, and
the Cane Fields; Their Duties and Salaries 29

CHAPTER VI: The Sugar Master, the Assistant Master
or *Banqueiro,* and the Assistant *Banqueiro* 33

CHAPTER VII: The Sugar Refiner 36

Contents

CHAPTER VIII: The Bookkeeper on the Plantation 37

CHAPTER IX: How the Planter Should Treat His Slaves 39

CHAPTER X: How the Planter Should Act in Directing
His Family and Ordinary Household Expenses 45

CHAPTER XI: How the Planter Should Receive Guests,
Whether Religious or Laymen 47

CHAPTER XII: How the Planter Should Deal with Merchants as
Well as with His Agents in the Market Place; Some of the Ways
of Buying and Selling Sugar, as Practiced in Brazil 49

BOOK 2

CHAPTER I: The Choice of Land on Which to Plant the Cane,
and for Supplying Provisions Needed for the Mill 53

CHAPTER II: Planting and Weeding Canes, and
the Different Kinds of Them 55

CHAPTER III: Enemies of the Cane in the Field 58

CHAPTER IV: Cutting the Cane and Carrying It to the Mill 60

CHAPTER V: The Mill, the Building Housing It,
and How Water Powers It 63

CHAPTER VI: How the Cane Is Milled and the
Number of People Required to Mill It 70

CHAPTER VII: The Wood Used to Make the Rollers, and All Other
Woodworking on the Plantation, Canoes and Boats, and What Is
Normally Paid to Carpenters and Similar Workers 73

CHAPTER VIII: Furnaces, Their Equipment, the Required
Firewood, and the Ash Used for Leaching 76

CHAPTER IX: The Cauldrons and Copper Vessels, Their
Organization, the Skilled Workers and Others
Required, and the Tools They Use 80

Contents

CHAPTER X: Cleaning and Purifying the *Caldo* from the
Cane in the Cauldrons and the Filtering Kettle until
It Reaches the Boiling Pans 84

CHAPTER XI: How *Melado* Is Cooked and
Whisked in the Boiling Pans 87

CHAPTER XII: The Three Temperings of *Melado* and
Its Correct Distribution in the Molds 89

BOOK 3

CHAPTER I: Regarding the Molds for Sugar and Their
Movement from the Cooling Shed to the Refinery 93

CHAPTER II: Refining the Sugar in Its Molds 95

CHAPTER III: The People Required to Refine, Separate,
Dry, and Crate the Sugar; the Tools Needed to Do This 97

CHAPTER IV: The Clay Used for the Sugar Molds; What Type
It Should Be, How It Should Be Kneaded, and If It Is Wise
to Have a Pottery Workshop on the Plantation 99

CHAPTER V: How Sugar Is Refined in the Molds
and How It Is Treated in the Refinery 101

CHAPTER VI: How Sugar Is Removed from
the Molds, Separated, and Dried 104

CHAPTER VII: Weighing, Distributing, and Crating the Sugar 107

CHAPTER VIII: Various Types of Sugar Crated Separately, the Marks
on the Crates, and Their Transport to the Warehouse 109

CHAPTER IX: The Past and Present Prices of Sugar 112

CHAPTER X: The Number of Crates of Sugar
Normally Produced Each Year in Brazil 114

CHAPTER XI: The Cost of a Crate of Sugar of Thirty-Five
Arrobas Cleared through the Customs House in Lisbon, and
the Value of All Sugar Produced in Brazil Each Year 115

CHAPTER XII: The Suffering of Sugar from the Time
It Is Born in the Field until It Leaves Brazil 118

Contents

THE SECOND PART

*The Development and Wealth of Brazil through
the Cultivation of Tobacco* 121

CHAPTER I: How Tobacco Was Developed in Brazil
and What Esteem It Has Attained 123

CHAPTER II: The Labor of Tobacco, How It Is Seeded,
Transplanted, and Weeded, and When to Plant It 125

CHAPTER III: How the Tobacco Leaves Are Picked and Cured
and How These Are Treated and Made into Coils 127

CHAPTER IV: How Tobacco Is Cured after Making Coils 129

CHAPTER V: How Tobacco Is Rolled and Encased
in Leather and Those Engaged in This Entire Process
from Planting until Rolling 130

CHAPTER VI: The Second and Third Collections
of Tobacco Leaves and Their Diverse Qualities for
Chewing, Smoking, or Grinding 132

CHAPTER VII: How Tobacco Is Ground, Sifted,
Powdered, and Perfumed 133

CHAPTER VIII: The Moderate Use of Tobacco for Health and the
Great Injury Done to the Health However It Is Used 134

CHAPTER IX: How Tobacco Is Cleared through
the Customs House of Bahia 136

CHAPTER X: The Cost of One Roll of Tobacco of Eight
Arrobas, Sent from Bahia to the Customs House in Lisbon,
with Duties Paid, Ready to Ship 137

CHAPTER XI: The High Regard in Which Brazilian Tobacco
Is Held in Europe and Other Parts of the World, and the Great
Tax Revenues It Provides the Royal Treasury 138

CHAPTER XII: The Penalties for Trafficking in Tobacco Not Cleared
through Customs and Methods Used to Avoid Taxation 140

Contents

THE THIRD PART
The Development and Wealth of Brazil by Gold Mining 143

CHAPTER I: The Gold Mines Discovered in Brazil 145

CHAPTER II: The Gold Mines Called "General"
and Who Discovered Them 147

CHAPTER III: The Other Gold Mines along the
Rio das Velhas and in Caeté 149

CHAPTER IV: The Yield from the Creeks and the Different
Qualities of Gold Extracted from Them 150

CHAPTER V: The People in the Mines and Who
Mine Gold in the Streams 152

CHAPTER VI: The Rights or Shares of the Mines 154

CHAPTER VII: The Great Availability of Equipment and
Daily Necessities in the Mines and the Indifference about
Their Extraordinarily High Prices 155

CHAPTER VIII: The Different Prices for Gold Sold in Brazil and
the Amounts of Gold Annually Extracted from the Mines 158

CHAPTER IX: The Obligation to Pay the King, Our Lord,
One-Fifth of the Gold Extracted from the Mines in Brazil 161

CHAPTER X: The Route from the Town of São Paulo to
the General Mines and to the Rio das Velhas 172

CHAPTER XI: The Old Route from the City of Rio de Janeiro to
the General Mines of Cataguás and the Rio das Velhas 176

CHAPTER XII: The New Route from the City of
Rio de Janeiro to the Mines 177

CHAPTER XIII: The Route from the City of Bahia
to the Mines of the Rio das Velhas 181

CHAPTER XIV: How Gold Is Extracted from the Mines and
Creeks in Brazil, as Observed by Someone Traveling
with Governor Artur de Sá 183

Contents

CHAPTER XV: How to Recognize Silver Mines 187

CHAPTER XVI: How to Recognize Silver and Purify Metals 189

CHAPTER XVII: The Damage Done to Brazil by Greed
Following the Discovery of Gold in Mines 192

THE FOURTH PART

*The Development and Wealth of Brazil by the
Abundance of Cattle, Leatherworking, and Other
Royal Contracts Remaining in This Colony* 195

CHAPTER I: The Great Expanses of Land for
Pastures in Brazil, Filled with Cattle 197

CHAPTER II: The Herds Normally Conducted from
Their Ranches to the Cities, Towns, and Bays of Brazil
Destined for Both the Slaughterhouse as well as Sugar Mills,
Tobacco Farms, and Other Places of Industry 202

CHAPTER III: Transporting Herds from the Interior, the Normal
Prices for Cattle for Slaughter and Cattle for Farmers 204

CHAPTER IV: The Cost of One Hide of Leather and
Half a Hide, Treated and Exported from Brazil,
Placed in the Lisbon Customs House 206

CHAPTER V: Summary of Everything Normally Exported
Annually from Brazil to Portugal and Its Value 207

THE LAST CHAPTER: How It Is Only Just that Brazil Is Favored
Because of Its Value to the Kingdom of Portugal 209

Notes 211

Glossary 219

Index 221

THERE IS NO BOOK that better captures the social and economic basis of Brazil in its early history than *Cultura e Opulência do Brasil por suas drogas e minas*, written by the Italian Jesuit Giovanni Antonio Andreoni (1649–1716) under the pseudonym André João Antonil. Andreoni had long experience in Brazil and held important administrative offices in the Jesuit order while he lived there, serving at different times as rector of the Jesuit College in Bahia and as provincial of the Jesuit order in Brazil. He operated in the highest circles of government as confessor to two governors of the colony and as advisor on legal and religious matters to the archbishop of Salvador. Exactly when he composed the book is not clear, but internal evidence suggests that Andreoni wrote it over a period from the 1690s to the first decade of the eighteenth century; it was published in Lisbon in 1711. Very few copies (only seven) of that first edition exist today because the Portuguese government immediately prohibited the book and removed it from circulation, nervous that it revealed too much about the routes to gold mines that had begun to produce in the late 1690s. The full text was not published again until 1837, long after the mines had played out. Since that time, historians and students of Brazil have been mining Antonil's text for the incredible wealth of details that it contains about the Brazilian economy and the slave-based society that developed around it.

Andreoni was an educated man. Born in Tuscany, in the city of Luca, he had studied civil law at the University of Perugia, and his talents as a lawyer, teacher, and as a Latinist eased his rise in the Jesuit order after he joined it in 1667. He had been working in Rome when he met the famous and combative Portuguese Jesuit preacher, missionary, and statesman António Vieira (1608–97). Vieira was considerably older than the Italian, but it was apparently that relationship that led Andreoni to seek a position in the Jesuit order in Brazil. They sailed together in 1683. Andreoni remained in Brazil for the rest of his life, rising in the Jesuit order and often taking positions contrary to those of his former sponsor

Vieira in matters regarding internal struggles over Indian liberty, the role of native Brazilians in the Jesuit order, and missionary activities.

Given his humanistic background and religious profession, it is not surprising that Andreoni's book reflects his broad education and certain moral and ethical concerns, but the heart of this book and its greatest value lies in the detailed and perceptive discussion of the primary economic activities of the Brazilian colony: sugar and tobacco agriculture, cattle raising and the production of hides, and mining. The *Cultura* of the title really refers to agriculture, and the models for the book that Andreoni seems to have used are classical works on Roman agriculture and rural life that had become popular in humanist circles in the seventeenth century. Andrée Mansuy, author of a definitive French translation and edition of Antonil's book, has suggested that, given the fact that more than half the book is devoted to the sugar industry and that the detail and literary style with which this section is written are distinct from those of the shorter and simpler sections of the rest of the work, it was Antonil's original intention to publish the part on sugar separately. This section was probably written in the mid-1690s, based on a ten-day visit Andreoni made to a large Jesuit-owned *engenho* (sugar mill) called Sergipe do Conde, located in the *Recôncavo* of Bahia, a center of the sugar industry where close to 150 mills were operating when Antonil made his visit. The remainder of the book was added between 1703 and 1707. This was the moment when the economy of Brazil, which had been built on sugar and tobacco cultivation and export, was now expanding as a result of the opening of the gold washings and mines in the south-central part of the colony, the area of Minas Gerais. From the organization of the book and from its contents, it appears that Andreoni wrote as an admirer and spokesman for the sugar industry that had been the backbone of the Brazilian economy for about a century, but that had gone through a difficult period in the 1670s and 1680s and was just recovering in the 1690s when the first gold strikes were made. A rush to the mines had ensued as farms and plantations were abandoned, slaves were shipped to the mining zone, prices rose, and agriculture was threatened. A governor of Brazil in that period warned the king that the true mines of Brazil were its farms and plantations, and Antonil seems to have agreed. The protagonists of his book are clearly the planters and the cane farmers (*lavradores*) who had become the social elite of the colony, and whose interests this book best represents.

The genius of Andreoni's book lies in the details he provides about the specifics of the activities he describes. His description of the planting, harvesting, milling, processing, crating, and shipping of sugar reads like a handbook for people in that industry with attention given to the tools and techniques, the mechanical problems, the scheduling, and the other minutia of operating an agro-industry. But Andreoni did not hesitate to embellish his minute descriptions and technical details with baroque literary metaphors and images, at one point even comparing the stages that sugarcane passed through in its processing to those of the purification of the soul. He gives advice on how to raise children, how to deal with lawyers, and how to treat one's neighbors.

Perhaps most important, much of his book is devoted to social roles and social relations, especially the proper and most advantageous comportment that a mill owner (*senhor do engenho*) should have with his workers, dependents, tenant cane farmers, slaves, family members, merchants, and God. In the text's very first sentence, Antonil makes clear that to be a sugar planter was not simply an occupation, but a status of power and command that he equated with a title of nobility in Portugal. He never questions the disparities of wealth and power of colonial society, nor does he ever doubt the validity of the slavery on which that society was based. Slavery is accepted as a legitimate if unfortunate institution, and while, as other Jesuit authors had done in Brazil, he admonishes slave owners to treat their slaves humanely, he bases that admonition both on Christian principles and on the practical advantages of such treatment. Masters are required to practice Christian charity, but servitude and obedience are required from slaves and subordinates.

Antonil's book is not a critique of colonial society, but rather a vivid description by an intelligent, meticulous, and perceptive insider of the economic foundations and the social patterns of Portuguese America. Through its pages pass not only sugar planters but also tobacco farmers, great cattle barons, merchants, and blacksmiths, slaves and freed people, mulattos, Portuguese immigrants, and African slaves, all of them seen primarily through a mercantilist lens.

Although small sections of *Cultura e opulência* have been available to Anglophone readers for many years, there has been no English-language edition of the complete text. The great English historian Charles Boxer began work on such a project in the 1960s but unfortunately abandoned it after Mansuy's excellent French translation and edition appeared. This volume now rectifies that situation. Anyone interested in early modern colonialism and in slave societies will learn a great deal from this book, and for an introduction to the social and economic structures of colonial Brazil and to the ideology that supported them, there is no better starting point than Antonil.

Stuart B. Schwartz
Yale University

INTRODUCTION

I N WRITING THIS WORK, Giovanni Antonio Andreoni decided not to use his real name, but rather signed the work "The Anonymous Tuscan," and André João Antonil. Andreoni was an Italian Jesuit born in 1649. After studying law, he entered the Jesuit order in 1667. He left for Portugal and in 1681 set sail for Brazil in the company of one of colonial Brazil's most famous Jesuits, Father António Vieira. Andreoni lived the rest of his life in Brazil. With the exception of several short visits to the north, he lived in Bahia, serving various roles at the Jesuit college there, including rector. He died there in 1716, only five years after this work was published. As the reader will quickly note, he was an astute observer of the world of sugar and tobacco in Bahia. He did not visit the gold mines that he describes, but tells us his information came from "someone traveling with Governor Artur de Sá." He may have seen many of the cattle areas he mentions, but since they are so widespread, it is doubtful he went to all the regions he outlines and must have depended on information he gathered in Bahia.

The publication history of this work, *Cultura e Opulência,* is dramatic. The book is a virtual how-to manual for making money in the Brazilian colony, focusing on sugar production, growing tobacco, gold mining (the three largest and most profitable economic activities at the time), and raising cattle (an activity that supported the other three). After first permitting its publication in 1711 (note the series of licenses that open the work), the Crown suppressed it. Royal authorities were very successful in doing so; only a handful of examples of the 1711 first edition exist. Two details contained in the book may have been responsible for making the royal authorities change their minds. First, the section on gold mining in great detail lists the routes from the coast to the interior gold fields, making these vulnerable to possible foreign intrusions.[1] Second, Antonil provides very detailed totals of the gross sales and net profits from each of these activities, which (from the Crown's perspective) could easily have been too much information to make public.

Written while the sugar boom and the discovery of large gold deposits were sweeping through colonial Brazil, the work would have to wait until the much later to be discovered and used by historians. In the nineteenth and twentieth centuries, it has been reprinted numerous times (1800, 1837, 1898, 1899, 1955, 1964, 1969, 1974, and 1982). It was translated into French by Andrée Mansuy in 1968 in an authoritative text with lengthy commentary and explanations of the people, places, and terms used in the original.[2]

The work is divided into three books on sugar, each consisting of twelve chapters. The first book is a general overview of the society sugar created and has some wonderful social insights and commentary. The second book details the production of sugar, while the third book deals with the packing, shipping, sale, costs, and profits made in sugar. Sugar is about half or more of the total work. Following it are what he calls "the second, third, and fourth parts." The first of these outlines the production of tobacco in twelve chapters. Gold mining is the third section, and it consists of seventeen chapters. The final part consists of four chapters on the cattle industry and includes a brief conclusion. The reader might wonder why cattle and oxen are included in the obviously lucrative enterprises of sugar, tobacco, and gold. Not only was cattle ranching profitable (as Antonil clearly shows in the last section), but cattle and oxen are tied to the other activities, since they provided power on the plantations and farms, encasing for the tobacco, and food for the plate.

While it is true that the work is very clearly focused on economic activities, there is also a great deal of social information contained in it. In Book 1, on sugar, we see Antonil's vision of how the planter should behave in this society where he is king. Antonil cautions the would-be planter to be vigilant regarding workmen and their expenses, generous in his dealings with his sharecroppers and other planters, watchful in the upbringing of his sons, thrifty in his expenses for entertainment, and firm but fair in his dealings with his slaves. In these and all other aspects, he constantly points to balance and avoiding extremes, drawing parallels between overheating the sugar and extreme swings in mood or temperament. Here and there we clearly hear the voice of the Jesuit, providing some moralistic advice, such as when he cautions the planter not to send his sons to school in the city without adequate supervision, since that "gives them the freedom to court vice and contract shameful diseases that cannot be cured easily." In discussing the need to weed around the sugar cane, he makes a connection between these early weeds and human vices: the "earliest vices are those that spoil good character."

The one and only exception to this economic focus of the work occurs at the very end of the sugar sections in Book 3, Chapter XII, "The Suffering of Sugar." This is a unique chapter in the work where he clearly compares the production and crating of sugar with the life and suffering of Christ. I will leave it to the reader to discover that section and make his or her own conclusions.

It is at the end of the gold section that the reader comes to realize one of Antonil's major objectives in writing this work. He opens with, "There is nothing so good that it cannot be accompanied by much evil because of its misuse." He then continues to develop his thesis that the discovery of gold has driven up the prices of virtually everything in the Brazilian colony (especially the cost for foodstuffs and slaves) and thus is responsible for the ruination of the sugar planters. He suggests that the Crown should intervene in the prices of slaves and sugar to keep these from rising further. Finally, at the very end of the work, he strongly suggests greater action and better administration from the Crown to rule more effectively. He underlines the importance of Crown officials needing to listen more attentively to complaints from sugar growers and others in the colony, and to addressing these complaints with greater speed. In other words, this work has three layers of text: the minute and detailed descriptions of the economic activities, the interspersed Jesuit pieces of advice about life, and finally the plea for better administration and appreciation on the part of the Crown for the growing importance of Brazil and its revenues.

Cultura e Opulência is the single most important source for understanding the economy of colonial Brazil, especially as it entered the eighteenth century. Sergio Buarque de Holanda, the eminent Brazilian historian of the colonial period, called it "Without a doubt the most detailed known description of the economic life of the colony and for that reason, an indispensable work for historians."[3] The Portuguese text has been repeatedly used by many historians of the period and is widely known and cited as a fundamental and revealing source for understanding Brazil's colonial economy. Tempting glimpses of short passages from this work have appeared in English. A very small section on the sugar planter was translated into English and appeared in Benjamin Keen's *Latin American Civilization*.[4] The chapter on how the planter should treat his slaves was translated and appears in *Children of God's Fire*, edited by Robert Conrad.[5] A small section on gold mining appeared in E. Bradford Burns, *A Documentary History of Brazil*.[6] However, in spite of its widely recognized importance, *Cultura e Opulência* has never appeared in an English translation.

It is significant that as important a historian of the Portuguese World as Charles Boxer must have shared this opinion of the work, since in January of 1961 he began translating it into English. He completed Book 1, on sugar, and the first four chapters of Book 2, or approximately one-fourth of the entire text. Unfortunately, he stopped his work, and his translation was never completed. Why he stopped is anyone's guess, but I would note three hints. Book 2, Chapter V (where he stopped), is by far the most difficult chapter in the entire text to render into English. It focuses on the details of how the water wheel and rollers interact in the mill. In 1962, one of his masterful works on Brazil appeared, *The Golden Age of Brazil*. He used Antonil as a major source for that work. Lastly, the very scholarly and authoritative French translation by Mansuy appeared in 1965. Whatever his reason for stopping, his notes sat in a file for many years at the Lilly Library of Indiana University. They might have remained there indefinitely but for the massive and authoritative biography completed on Charles Boxer by Professor Dauril Alden.[7] In his work, Alden added a very interesting appendix of projects Boxer planned or started but never finished. This partial translation caught my attention. I immediately thought that a translation of such a fundamental work on colonial Brazilian history started by such an important figure as Boxer should be completed and published without delay.

It was for all of these reasons that the editorial team agreed that this work should appear in the new series of translations launched by Tagus Press at the University of Massachusetts Dartmouth. The series, Classic Histories from the Portuguese-Speaking World in Translation, will include a number of carefully selected texts in their first English translations.

A Note on the Translation

Boxer's translation was very much a first draft. He had been concentrating on translating the original phrase by phrase and had not yet started any grammatical transformation into English sentences. A good sentence in Portuguese is hopeless in English. It is unclear, flowery, redundant, and filled with run-on constructions. The process of changing Portuguese syntax and sentence structure into English is a tricky one. Nevertheless, Boxer's initial effort greatly accelerated the ultimate completion of this work. The reader should be aware that I have trimmed some redundant vocabulary here and there and have added understood words as needed to make the translation clearer and to allow it to flow more naturally in English. Whenever possible, I have made only minimal changes, especially to the first quarter of the work, translated by Charles Boxer. On a couple of rare occasions, I had to drop the original wording completely and do my best to state the author's meaning in English. For example, at one point Antonil describes the increase in demand for tobacco in Lisbon as growing from a "nursery of desires." There is no way to hammer that into English except to ask what the author means and reword it: "quickly became a success, stimulated demand. . . ." My overall objective was to make the text readable in modern English, with minimal reference to footnote explanations. As Antonil himself states in his preface, he wrote thi`s work not in an attempt to create great literature but to describe in detail the economic activities in Brazil using "the same style and manner of speaking clearly and plainly, as they do in the sugar mills." Throughout the work he sticks to that standard, with the one very notable exception of the last chapter of sugar in Book 3. I cannot help but believe he would have approved of a straightforward and readable translation. The English text that follows is in the exact order as in the 1711 original, with the same paragraphs, with only one minor change. I have moved the "index" from the back of the work to the table of contents, to allow for easier reference.

A number of specialized dictionaries and references made this work possible.[8] Some of the terms used in these industries have no modern English equivalents, so I have retained these original terms. They are listed in a glossary for easy reference.

Acknowledgments

My students proved excellent allies in writing this translation. I was fortunate to have two classes of students read and comment on drafts of this translation, and their comments helped considerably. My colleague at the College of Charleston, Dr. Christophe Boucher, was most helpful in explaining the meaning of passages from the modern French translation, which I turned to from time to time. Special thanks to Professor James Gordley of Tulane University for translating several legal passages from Latin, as well as for his comments and explanations used in Chapter IX of the section on gold.

I would like to extend thanks to the director and staff of the Lilly Library for allowing me to use Boxer's draft. I am also very grateful to Ms. Carola Vecchio and Professor Boxer's estate for granting permission to publish his section of this translation.

I would also like to thank the John Carter Brown Library for allowing the use of the images for this work, and the Institute des Hautes Études de l'Amerique Latine for allowing the use of some of the maps created for the French translation.

This first English translation of *Cultura e Opulência do Brasil por suas drogas e minas* is respectfully dedicated to Stuart B. Schwartz, George Burton Adams Professor of History at Yale University and former professor of history at the University of Minnesota. Teacher, mentor, and a prolific and insightful historian of colonial Brazil, as well as Spanish America, Stuart has worked with numerous graduate students over the course of his many years of teaching. It was my great privilege to have been one of them. His students and numerous publications have been responsible for shaping and guiding the field of colonial Latin

American history, particularly colonial Brazil. No author is more closely linked to and more knowledgeable about the history of sugar, the masters and slaves who made it, and the colonial Brazilian society in which they lived.

Timothy J. Coates
The College of Charleston
Charleston, South Carolina

BRAZIL AT THE DAWN OF
THE EIGHTEENTH CENTURY

This copy is in agreement with the original. The Convent of Santissima Trinidade of Lisbon, March 5, 1711.

Father Manoel da Conceição

This copy agrees with the original and can be distributed. Lisbon, March 5, 1711.

Moniz.   Hasse.   Monteyro.   Ribeiro.   Rocha.
Fr. Encarnção.   Barreto.

To the gentlemen planters and producers of sugar and tobacco,
and to those engaged in mining gold in the state of Brazil.

B RAZIL OWES so much to the venerable Father Joseph de Anchieta,[1] one of the first and most fervent missionaries of this Southern America. This country enthusiastically calls him its great apostle and new miracle worker. It is through the light of the Gospel that he communicated to so many thousands of Indians, through the innumerable miracles that he worked during his lifetime and which he continues to work. His name is being continually invoked for the benefit of all. However, to confess these obligations without actively cooperating in exalting the glories of such a worthy benefactor, is not sufficient to express a true gratitude which is both due and expected. In order, therefore, to arouse this pious affection in the minds of all those who can more easily, thankfully, and liberally help such a holy work as is the canonization of such an illustrious man, I sought to accompany this petition with some gift. This might be both pleasing and useful to those who are experiencing Divine favor through the noteworthy increase of their worldly wealth in the sugar plantations, in the tobacco fields, and in the gold mines. Therefore, with this modest offering, I seek to stimulate that generous liberality which does not sanction being asked, for fear lest in giving it might seem as if it were selling benefits. To the said Venerable Father Joseph de Anchieta, I earnestly beg that he would seek from God a hundredfold recompense on earth and in heaven for whoever resolves to promote his honors with some alms. These honors, when proclaimed in the churches and celebrated on the altars, will likewise add greater glory to that Lord, who is honored in the honors paid to saints and glorified in their glories.

THE FIRST PART

The Agricultural Wealth of Brazil in the Cultivation of Sugar

A royal sugar mill in full production deals with:

The owner of the sugar mill, the overseers, and other hands who are occupied there, their duties and salaries;

The milling, building, workshops of the sugar mill, and what work is done in each of them;

The cultivation of the sugarcane, its transportation, and milling; how the sugar is refined and packed in the Bay of Bahia in Brazil for export to the Kingdom of Portugal and the profits derived from it.

[PREAMBLE]

W HOEVER FIRST CALLED the mills, wherein the sugar is made, *engenhos* made a true choice in the name.[1] For anyone who sees and thinks about them with the reflection they merit must necessarily confess that they are some of the chief products and inventions of human ingenuity, which, being a small portion of the Divine, always shows itself admirable in its way of working.

Some of the mills are called royal and others are commonly called *engenhocas*.[2] The royals got this name because they have all the requisite component parts and all the well-fitted workshops. They are manned by a large number of slaves, and are provided with many cane fields of their own, besides others whose produce is brought to them for milling, and principally because they have the grandeur of milling with water-power. In contrast, the others, which mill with horses and oxen, are less well provided and equipped. At any rate these latter have smaller and less perfect workshops, and only a small number of slaves to run a mill in full production.

One day, I thought I would like to see one of the most famous mills on the Bay of Bahia, called the Mill of Sergipe do Conde. Moved by a praiseworthy curiosity, during the eight or ten days that I stayed there, I tried to take notice of everything that was done in such a celebrated and virtual king of the royal sugar mills. I derived a great deal of information from the man who had administered the mill for more than thirty years with great intelligence and with all he learned over those years. I also learned from the experience of the famous sugar master, who had occupied this post for fifty years with fortunate results, and from other reputable officers, whom I questioned minutely about what pertained to each of them. I resolved to put down everything in this draft, which I compiled hurriedly but accurately in that short space of time. I did so in the same style and manner of speaking clearly and plainly, as they do in the sugar mills. This I did, so that those who do not know what the sweetness of the sugar costs to he who cultivates it, should know it, and thereby feel less bothered by paying what it is worth. Likewise, whoever begins to operate a sugar plantation should have this practical information drawn up to help him work skillfully, which is desirable in any occupation. For better order and clarity, I divided all the matters which pertain to this substance into various chapters, including the jobs of all those who work in and for its production. I began by relating the duties of each one, from the origin of sugar in the field, and ended with its final perfection in the chests. I did this with my modest stock of knowledge. At least this will serve to stimulate others who are better qualified and have more ready pens, to perfect this beginning. If anyone wants to know who is the author of this curious and useful work, he is a friend of the public good called

The Anonymous Tuscan

LICENSES OF THE HOLY OFFICE

Most Illustrious Sir

I INSPECTED this book entitled *Cultura e Opulência do Brasil,* mentioned in the above petition, and since it is a work of ingenuity owing to the methodical way in which the author has composed it, it is very deserving of the license which he asks. For by this means those who wish to emigrate to the State of Brazil will realize the great cost of cultivating sugar, tobacco, and searching for gold, which are sweeter to possess in this kingdom than to cultivate in Brazil. This book contains nothing contrary to our Holy Faith and good morals, and on this account it could be printed in letters of gold. This is my opinion, which I place at the feet of Your Eminence, so that you may order as you think best. Santa Anna of Lisbon, 8 November 1710.

Fr. Paulo de São Boaventura

THIS TREATISE has nothing suspect against our Holy Faith and the purity of good morals, and thus Your Eminence is well served and can concede the license for which the author asks. Trinidade, 30 November 1710.

Fr. Manoel da Conceição

IN VIEW OF the foregoing information, the book called *Cultura e Opulência do Brasil* can be printed and after once published must be returned for checking and the issue of the publication license, without which it may not be published. Lisbon, 5 December 1710.

Moniz. Hasse. Monteiro. Ribeiro.
Fr. Encarnação. Rocha. Barreto.

BOOK ONE

CHAPTER I

The Resources a Royal Sugar Mill Owner Should Possess

To BE A SUGAR PLANTER is a title to which many people aspire. It brings with it the service, the obedience, and the respect of many others. If he is, as he ought to be, a man of wealth and command, a sugar planter in Brazil can be esteemed proportionally to the titled nobility in the Kingdom of Portugal. There are some sugar mills in Bahia that yield the owner four thousand loaves of sugar, and others a little less. This figure includes the cane from tenants which has to be pressed in the mill, and to which the mill is entitled to at least half, as well as that which is pressed with no obligation.[1] In some other places in Brazil the mill receives even more than half.

Tenants depend on the planters. They rent fields on the lands belonging to the mill, as citizens do from nobles. When the planters are wealthier and have all the necessary provisions and are good-natured and truthful, then they are all the more sought after as landlords. This is true even for those who do not have their cane held captive, either by long-standing obligation or for the price that they receive for it.

Slaves serve the sugar planter with various functions with hoes and sickles, which he keeps on the plantation and in the mill. He is also served by mulattoes and *negros,* both male and female, occupied in household duties or in other jobs such as boatmen, canoe men, caulkers, carpenters, ox cart drivers, potters, cowboys, herdsmen, and fishermen. Each of these planters is also bound to have a sugar master, a *banqueiro,* an assistant *banqueiro,*[2] a refiner, a bookkeeper on the plantation and another in the city, overseers in the fields and allotments and a head overseer of the plantation, as well as chaplains for the spiritual side, and each one of these employees receives wages.

All the slaves (who on the larger plantations exceed 150 or 200 *peças*[3] including those in the fields) need food and clothing, medicines, an infirmary, and a man to care for the sick. For their sustenance, they need allotments with many thousand holes to plant cassava.[4] The boats require sails, cables, cordage, and pitch. The furnaces, which burn day and night during seven or eight months of the year, require a great deal of firewood. For this purpose, two sailing boats are needed to seek firewood in the ports, one replacing the other without stopping, and a lot of money to buy the wood. Alternatively, the planter requires large woods, with many carts and many yokes of oxen to transport the firewood. The cane fields also require their boats, and carts with doubled teams of oxen, hoes, and sickles. The sawmills require saws and axes. The mill demands a great stock of every kind of suitable wood and many *quintals* of steel and iron.[5] The carpenter's workshop needs strong, select woods for props, beams, sail-beams, and wheels. It also needs at least the more common tools such as saws, augers, piercers, compasses, rulers, chisels, adzes, gouges, axes, hammers, rabbet planes, jointers, nails, and joiner planes. The refinery requires tubs, cauldrons, kettles, and basins, and many other smaller utensils, all of copper, whose cost exceeds eight thousand *cruzados*,[6] even when they are sold cheaper than in these recent years. Finally, in addition to the slaves' quarters and the houses of the chaplain, the overseers, master, refiner, *banqueiro,* and bookkeeper, the estate needs a decent chapel with its ornaments and all the furnishings for the altar. It also needs a house for the sugar planter, with a separate room for guests, who visit very frequently in Brazil, where there are no inns whatsoever. Finally, the mill owner needs a strong and spacious building for the mill, together with other workshops, a refinery, an office, and a still. The plantation also needs other less important things, which need not be enumerated here, and will be discussed in their proper place.

Duly considering all this, some men of sufficient wealth and good judgment prefer to be substantial tenants of sugarcane, with one or two large fields of sugar. Each of these produces a thousand loaves of sugar, with twenty or forty slaves of the hoe and sickle. Some men prefer this than to be sugar planters for a few years, with all the trouble and worry which the management of such an estate demands. Considering all this, it is astonishing how many people nowadays boldly build small mills as soon as they have a fair number of slaves and can find someone to lend them a considerable sum of money. With this, they begin an undertaking for which they are not fit for lack of ability and means. It is all the more astonishing considering that they become so deeply indebted after the first harvest that they declare themselves bankrupt after the second or third. Likewise, they cause those who lent them money and equipment on trust also to go bankrupt. Meanwhile, others laugh at their ill-grounded presumption, which so quickly changed into dry straw from that first green glimmer of a promising but deceitful hope.

Even though not all the mills may be royal ones, nor need such vast expenses as we have outlined above, every owner experiences death and desertion among the slaves. All owners also face the loss of many horses and oxen, droughts that come unexpectedly and wither the cane, and frequent mishaps. With all these setbacks, costs are bound to be greater than what was anticipated. Consider also how the masons, carpenters, and other skilled craftsmen, desirous of profiting at another's expense, will frame their estimates in such a way that it will seem to him as easy to build the sugar mill as the slave quarters. When he has begun to assemble all the equipment, he will find that he has already spent everything he had before placing one stone upon another. He will have nothing left to pay the salaries, while the expenses will suddenly rise, as rivers do after floods of rain.

Likewise, he must have the ability, skill, and diligence necessary for the good management and organization of everything concerning the selection of overseers and skilled workers. He must also maintain good relations with the tenants, handle the slaves and subordinates, and supervise the upkeep and cultivation of the lands that he owns. In addition, he must deal promptly and honestly with merchants and his agents in the town. If he is not able to do these things he will only find disappointment and ignominy in the title of sugar planter, from which he expected so much credit and prestige. For this reason, having already spoken of what pertains to the wealth he should have, I will now deal with how he should manage his estate. I will begin with the purchase and upkeep of his lands, and those he leases to tenants. Then I will deal with the selection of the skilled workers he employs, noting their duties and the salaries paid to each one, according to the style of the royal sugar mills of Bahia. At the end, I will discuss the management of his family, children, and slaves, the reception of his guests, and the promptness with which he should satisfy his debts, on which depends the conservation of his credit, which is the best treasure of those who pride themselves on being honorable men.

How the Sugar Planter Should Act in the Purchase, Upkeep, and Leasing of His Lands

I F THE SUGAR PLANTER does not know the qualities of different soils, he will buy *saloens* soil instead of *massapé*, and *areiscas* rather than *salones*.[7] He should therefore avail himself of the advice of the most intelligent tenants and consider not only the cheapness of the price but likewise all the facilities that he needs to have a plantation with cane. These include pastures, water, allotments, and woods. If lacking forests, he will require firewood as nearby as possible. Old hands can point out to him other drawbacks to avoid. They are the masters taught by time and experience, of which young men are ignorant.

Many sell their lands because they are unproductive or lack firewood. Others do so because they cannot bear to hear as many sad tidings as were given to Job, such as of a burned field, of oxen stuck in the mire, of dead slaves, and of ruined sugar. Others, who are obligated to sell against their will owing to pressure applied by their creditors, may well offer new and fertile lands, but the buyer then runs the risk of being involved in unending lawsuits, owing to the encumbrances and mortgages to which they are repeatedly subjected. In such a case, the buyer should take legal advice and ask the creditors what they want, and if necessary summon them all through judicial authority to discover what they claim. He should not conclude the purchase until he has inspected the property with his own eyes, until he has seen what title deeds the seller has, and if the lands are entailed or freehold. He should also inquire if orphans, monasteries, or churches have some share in the lands, so that no critical provision or formality is absent when the deed of sale is drawn up. He should also ascertain whether the boundaries of the lands were demarcated correctly according to the law, and if the boundary markers are in place or need replacing. What sort of people are the other inheritors? That is to say, are they law-abiding, truthful, and peaceful, or, on the contrary, are they dishonest, unruly, and violent? There is no worse plague than a bad neighbor.

When the sale is made, he must not fail to keep his given word, and to pay promptly what he owes at the agreed time. He should maintain and improve what he has bought, and above all use every means to protect the boundary markers and waterways which he needs to drive his mill. He must show his children and overseers these boundary markers, so they know what belongs to them, and they can avoid legal demands and actions. These are continual vexations to the soul and cause rivers of money to bleed into the households of advocates, solicitors, and clerks. After so many expenses and disappointments, they bring little gain to a plaintiff, even if he wins. Nor should he leave his legal papers and deeds in his wife's trunk, or on a table exposed to dust, wind, white ants, and moth worms. Keeping papers in a safe place will avoid being compelled to offer many Masses to Saint Anthony, in order to find some important paper that could not be found when it was needed.[8] For it might happen that the maid or female slave took three or four sheets of paper from her mistress's trunk in order to wrap up something she wanted. The smallest child might likewise have taken some sheets of paper off the table, in order to paint masks or to make paper boats for flies and crickets to sail in. Finally, the wind might have caused them to fly without feathers out of the house.

In order to have tenants who are obliged to press their cane in the mill, it is necessary to give them leaseholds of the land they are to plant. These leases commonly run for nine years, with one year for removal, and with the obligation to leave planted so many *tarefas* of cane.[9] Or, they run for eighteen years or more, with the obligation to plant as many *tarefas* as is agreed in conformity with the regional practice. However, care should be taken to ensure that those who ask for leaseholds are industrious farmers and not those who would bring its ruin, so that they will be profitable and not harmful. Care must be taken to insert the necessary conditions in the lease, such as that they may not cut down the Crown's trees, that they should not sublet their leaseholds to others without the permission of the owner, and other such clauses necessary to prevent one of the bolder tenants turning himself into a planter. For this reason, it would be a good precaution to have a set form or record of the leaseholds drawn up by one of the more experienced lawyers, stipulating what should be done regarding improvements during the time of removal, so that the end of the lease does not mean the beginning of eternal lawsuits.

How the Planter Should Deal with Tenants and His Other Neighbors and They with Him

OFTEN, WHEN rich and powerful men come to possess consider-able wealth, it also brings feelings of contempt for more noble people. For this reason, God often deprives them of their wealth so that they should not avail themselves of it to increase their pride. Whoever comes to secure the title of planter is apt to try and treat all his subordinates as slaves. This is chiefly seen in some planters who have tenants on the lands belonging to the mill, or tenants who are obliged to have their cane pressed there, treating them with haughtiness and arrogance. It follows that such planters are generally disliked and criticized by those who cannot endure them, and that many of these latter rejoice at the losses and disasters that unexpectedly overtake the former. These downtrodden wretches are continually imploring God for justice, see-ing themselves so oppressed and desiring their oppressors be brought low so that they should learn not to mistreat the humble. This is the same as when the physician tries to draw out the malignant and surplus evil humors which make the body indisposed and sick, so as to give it in this way not only life but likewise perfect health.[10]

The planter should therefore have nothing of pride, arrogance, and haughtiness about him. On the contrary, he should be good-natured toward all, and look on his tenants as true friends. This is what they really are when they make every effort to keep their cane fields weeded and well planted for the great profit of the mill. He should give them all the help he can in their difficulties, both with his authority and with his estate. Nor should he be less careful to be very just and upright when the time comes to press the cane in the mill and to make and pack the sugars. For it would not be right for him to take for himself the days for milling which he should give to the tenants in their turn. He should also not give more days to one tenant than to another, or mix the sugar that is being made for one tenant with that from one *tarefa* of another. Nor should he choose the best sugar for himself and give the tenant the inferior. In order to avoid these failings or any other suspect practices, he should inform or communicate in good time with whoever's turn is next, so that he can cut and transport the cane and have it in the mill on the appointed day. This will allow him to have his mark on the molds, so that they can be distinguished from the others. Nor should he object if the tenants want to see their sugar in the cooling shed, in the refinery, in the gallery, or in the packing place. It has cost them so much to get it in this state, and so much bitterness has preceded this modest sweetness.

Likewise, it will show that he is ill disposed if he makes himself unpleasant to those who have their sugar pressed in other mills merely because the cane is free of any obligation and they choose not have it pressed in his own mill. Nor should he be on bad terms with other planters merely because any of them press as much cane as another, or because things go better for one or another of them, with less expense and without losses. If the envy between the first brothers in the world came to such a pitch that it reddened the hands of Cain with the blood of Abel, because Abel had received the blessing of Heaven and Cain had not, through the latter's own fault, who can doubt but that similar tragedies may be reenacted among relatives even today? For are there not many regions in Brazil where the sugar planters are closely related to each other by blood and little united in charity? Self-interest is the sole origin of their discord, and perchance it suffices to cut down a tree or that a stray ox enters a cane field for the hidden hatred to flare up and to institute deadly lawsuits and feuds. The sole way, therefore, of a planter avoiding serious vexations, is to behave with all urbanity and distinction, politely asking for anything that it may be necessary to borrow from neighbors, and furthermore, to convince himself that if they refuse to give what is requested, this is only because they cannot spare it. Even when he realizes that the refusal is for lack of generosity, the true and noblest vengeance will be on the first occasion when this same person makes a request. He should promptly give double what is requested to he who initially refused to loan. In this way, the latter will be shown gracefully how he ought to behave.

Above all, those who ought to behave with the greatest respect toward the planter are the tenants who have fields whose produce must be pressed in his mill. Even more respect should come from those who cultivate the lands the planter has leased to them, especially when this sort of people begin their working lives modestly and eventually became well to do. Ingratitude and lack of the respect and courtesy due in such circumstances is a fault worthy of severe censure, while a humble thankfulness binds the souls of all men with chains of gold. However, this respect must never be carried so far that it becomes a readiness to act unjustly, chiefly when a man might be asked to do something contrary to God's law, such as giving false evidence on oath in criminal cases or lawsuits, or to show hatred to persons who might stand up for themselves. What I have said of the planters applies equally to their wives, who should be treated with greater deference than others. However, they should not presume to be treated like queens, nor that the wives of the tenants ought to be their servants, or that they appear among them as the moon among the smaller stars.

How the Planter Should Behave in Choosing the Hands and Skilled Workers He Engages, Beginning with the Choice of Chaplain

I F THERE IS ONE THING above all others in which the planter should show his capacity and wisdom, it is without doubt in the good choice of the hands and skilled workers whom he takes into his service for the smooth running of the plantation. Since choice is the daughter of prudence, he can rightly be condemned as unwise who chooses reprobates, or those unfitted for what they have to do. It is obvious that good-for-nothings will be displeasing to God and to men, and will be the cause of many and serious vexations; others through their ineptitude will cause excessive damage to the estate. The planter can rightly be blamed for this, not only by his own family, who will be the first burned or singed by his behavior, but likewise those outside, and especially the tenants. They will be inadvertently compelled to suffer the losses resulting from their unrequited toil if the skilled workers do not know their respective jobs.

The first to be hired is the chaplain. He should be chosen with circumspection and after obtaining secret information regarding his comportment and knowledge. He is entrusted with teaching everything concerning the Christian ways of life. In this way, he will be able to fulfill the most important of his duties, which are catechizing and instructing the household and the slaves. He can do this, and it will not be done through a local slave or an overseer, who at the most can teach them verbally some prayers and the Ten Commandments. He will be someone who knows how to explain to them what they must believe, how they must believe, and how to pray to God for what they need. If it should be necessary for this reason to give the chaplain something more than the average stipend, the planter may rest assured that good money could not be placed in better hands.

The chaplain, then, has the duty of saying Mass in the plantation chapel on Sundays and Holy Days. This leaves him free to say Mass on the other days of the week for whoever wishes this, save only if he makes another kind of contract with the owner of the chapel, receiving a stipend proportional to his work. On the said Sundays and Holy Days, or at least on the Sundays, if he is engaged on this condition, he will expound the catechism. That is to say, he will explain the principal mysteries of the faith, and the commandments of God and the Holy Church:

† What a great evil is mortal sin, and what punishment God has ordained for it in this and in the next life, where the soul lives and will live for all eternity.

† What remedy God has given us in the incarnation and death of Jesus Christ, his most holy son, so that our sins may be forgiven, as likewise the penances we must undergo to pay for our sins.

† In what way we should confess our sins, and ask God to pardon them, with true repentance and the firm resolve never to commit them again, with the help of divine grace.

† In what manner we make penitence for our sins.

† Who is in the most Holy Sacrament on the altar?

† Why He is there and who receives Him.

† In what frame of mind the sacrament should be taken in life and the *viaticum*[11] when on the point of death.

† How important it is to gain indulgences, so as to discount something from what has to be paid in Purgatory.

† How everyone has to commit himself to God so as not to fall into sin, and how He should be offered in the morning the work of the ensuing day.

† How abominable are the witch doctors and folk healers who use words to heal, and those who resort to them, abandoning God from whom all salvation comes. Equally evil are those who give poison or drinks (as they say) in order to influence or sway the minds. So are drunkards, fornicators, thieves, seekers of revenge, gossip-mongers, and those who bear false witness, either from malice or greed of gain, or for worldly reasons.

† And finally, what reward and what punishment God will give
eternally to each one according to his behavior in this life.

The chaplain must also seek approval from higher religious authority
to hear the confession of his penitents, so that in his capacity as priest
and minister of God he can often be of help to them, not contenting
himself merely with extreme unction[12] to those who are dying. But
he must remember in administering the Last Sacrament that he is not
the lord thereof, however great his authority. For if the penitent is not
in the right frame of mind, owing to his living in concubinage,[13] or
bearing hatred to his neighbors, or through not being resolved to make
restitution of good name or money which he owes, then even if he is
the sugar planter himself, he cannot receive absolution. In such a case,
for human respects, there may well be a heavily burdened conscience
and a very serious moral responsibility.

The chaplain is likewise responsible for making peace between everyone, and preventing quarrels. He must ensure that God is duly honored in the chapel that he serves, and likewise Our Lady the Virgin,
whose litany must be sung on Saturdays, and the *Terce* of the Rosary[14]
in the months when the mill is not running. He must forbid laughter,
conversation, and indecent practices, not only in the chapel but also
in the entry hall, particularly when the holy sacrifice of Mass is being
celebrated.

He must further not proclaim the banns,[15] nor baptize anyone except
in an emergency, nor hear confessions or give the sacrament during
Lent[16] without the written permission of the vicar who is authorized to
give it. Nor can he do anything that infringes on the jurisdiction of the
parish priests, lest he incur the penalties and censures that are decreed
for this, and he will vainly complain of his ignorance and carelessness.

Finally, he must insist on living outside the planter's house, for this
is a convenience for both of them. He is a priest and not a servant;
he is a familiar of God and not of other men. Nor should he have a
female slave for his service, unless she is elderly, nor should he act as a
merchant of either spiritual or worldly things, because all this is very
contrary to the clerical state to which he professes, and is forbidden to
him by the decrees of the various Supreme Pontiffs.[17]

The sum usually given to a chaplain for his work, when he is free for saying the weekday Mass, is forty or fifty *milréis*.[18] This and what the penitents give him amounts to a sufficient stipend, fairly earned, provided that he keeps the rules listed above. If he has to instruct the sons of the planter, then he should be given a larger sum that is fair payment for the additional work.

On the day in which the milling of the cane begins, if the planter does not ask the vicar to officiate, then the chaplain will bless the mill and pray God to give it a good yield and to free all those who work there from any kind of harm. When the mill stops working at the end of the harvest, he must encourage everyone to attend a thanksgiving service in the chapel.

CHAPTER V

The Head Overseer and the Subordinate Overseers
Who Preside in the Milling, the Estate, and the
Cane Fields; Their Duties and Salaries

THE OVERSEERS ARE the planter's arms for the good administration of his estate and people. However, if each one wants to be boss, then that administration will become a monster, a true likeness of the dog Cerberus, whom the poets fabulously endowed with three heads. I do not say that authority should not be given to the overseers, but I do say that this authority must be well regulated and subordinate, not absolute. The lesser should be subordinate to the higher, and all of them to the planter whom they serve. It is desirable that the slaves should be convinced that the head overseer has great authority to order, to reprimand, and to punish them when necessary. However, this should be done in such a way that they likewise know that they can appeal to the planter, and that he will give them a just hearing. Nor should the other overseers, just because they are endowed with authority, believe that they have unlimited and boundless power to imprison and punish slaves. For this reason, the planter should clearly state exactly what authority he gives to each of them, and give more to the head overseer. If they exceed these limits, he should rebuke them sharply with the reprimand that their excesses deserve, but not in front of the slaves, because they might, at a later time, become insubordinate to the overseer. He will resent being reprimanded in front of them and lose his confidence in ordering them about. It will be sufficient if the planter, through a third person, informs the slave who suffered (and some of the more senior ones on the estate) that the overseer was severely reprimanded for the fault which he committed and was told that if he would not mend his ways, he would certainly be dismissed.

On no account should the overseer be allowed to kick the slaves, especially not the stomachs of pregnant women. Nor should they be allowed to strike slaves with a stick, for in their anger they do not count their blows and they thus may inflict a mortal injury on the head of a very valuable slave and cause his death. On the other hand, the overseer may well be allowed when necessary to reprimand the slaves and to teach them by giving them a few lashes on the back with a stick. Moreover, it is a good thing for him to imprison runaways, those who wound each other by fighting, or those who get drunk, so that the planter may later order them to be punished, as they deserve. However, under no circumstances whatever should the overseer be allowed to tie up a slave and whip him until the blood runs. Nor should an overseer be allowed to place a slave in chains for months on end (when the planter is away in the city), such as when a female slave refuses him the use of her body. Also, the overseer cannot be allowed to falsely accuse a male slave who gives a truthful account of the disloyalty, brutality, and cruelty of the overseer. To condone such proceedings would be to employ a ravenous wolf and not a Christian and temperate overseer.

It is the duty of the head overseer to control the people on the plantation and to allot them their various tasks as required for the service of the estate. It is his job to learn from the planter whom he should tell to cut their cane and without delay to send each a message to that effect. He must also prepare the boats and the carts to transport the cane, the molds, and the firewood. He must give the planter a list of everything needed for the functioning of the mill before it begins to operate. As soon as the harvest is finished, he must see that everything is put away in its place. He must ensure that nobody fails in his duty. He must be ready to intervene at once when any accident happens, so as to remedy it as much as possible. When a slave falls ill, he should excuse him from work and put another in his place. He should also tell the planter so that he can have the sick man cured, and the chaplain so that he can hear his confession, or comfort him with the sacraments in the face of death, if the illness gets worse. He must take care not to yoke in the carts oxen that have been heavily worked in the preceding days. Just as some rest must be given to the oxen and horses, so with greater reason must the slave gangs be allowed to rest from time to time.

The overseer in charge of the milling, at the proper time, must summon the female slaves to collect the cane, and he must see that it is inserted properly in the rollers and the crushed stalks are removed. He must watch carefully to see that the female slaves do not fall asleep. This is because of the danger, if they do, of their being caught and crushed if their hands are not cut off to free them. If this happens, the overseer must likewise have the water diverted from the wheel so that the mill stops. He must try to ensure that the rollers are washed every twenty-four hours and that the juice is clean and brought to the vat. He must ask how much juice is needed in the cauldrons, so that he will then know to order more cane to be milled or to have the machine stopped until it is drained, so as to avoid having the juice already in the vat turn sour.

The overseers who are in the cane fields and other parts of the estates are responsible for guarding the lands. They must immediately inform the planter if anyone enters the allotments, cane fields, or woods to take that which is not his. They must be present where the slaves are working, so as to see that they do their duties properly. They must know the right time to plant, weed, cut the cane, and cultivate the allotments. They should know the qualities of the different soils so as to make the best use of them for whatever they will grow. They must extract from each slave the tasks and the loads he or she is obliged to fulfill. The overseer must see that the cart tracks are in good enough condition so that the cane and firewood can be transported without becoming stuck in the mud. He must see that every slave has his sickle and hoe and whatever else he needs for his work. He must also take great care that the cane fields are not set on fire through the carelessness of the new slave hands, who sometimes throw into the wind the firebrand that they carry to light their pipes. When he sees any blaze, he must go there at once with all the people he can muster and cut a swath in the path of the advancing fire, which otherwise might easily destroy in half an hour many *tarefas*[19] of cane.

Although it is known what *tarefa* of cane the average *negro* can plant or cut in a day, how many holes of cassava he can plant or reap, and what load of firewood he can gather, as will be said in due course, the overseer must consider the age and strength of each slave. This will allow him to lighten the daily task of those who obviously cannot do so much, such as women who are more than six months pregnant, those who have recently given birth and are nursing mothers, old men and women, and those who are still recovering after a severe illness.

The head overseer in a royal mill gets sixty *milréis*. The overseer of a mill operating for seven or eight months receives forty or fifty *milréis*, particularly if he has some other job as well; where there is less to do and he has no additional job, only thirty *milréis*. The overseers who supervise work in the cane fields and other parts of the estate where the work is heavy are also nowadays paid at the rate of forty or fifty *milréis*.

CHAPTER VI

The Sugar Master, the Assistant Master or
Banqueiro, *and the Assistant* Banqueiro

HE WHO MAKES THE sugar is rightly termed the master; his work needs intelligence, application, and experience. Moreover, any kind of experience is not enough, but it must be local, so that he knows the place and the quality of the cane. He must know where it should be planted and milled, for the cane fields in some localities yield a very strong cane and in others a very weak one. The juice from the lowland cane is different from that grown on the hillsides. Lowland cane is very watery and the boiled juice needs a lot of refining in the cauldrons. Hillside cane is sweeter, and the juice takes less time to boil and fewer ashes for its refining and crystallization. Some kinds of sugarcane juice require more cooking than others. One type will quickly thicken in the cooking pans, while another will be slower. The three stages of boiling the juice, required in order to use the molds, depend on how well or poorly the refining of the sugar is done. If the master trusts the boilers and men stirring the cauldrons, he will find that sometimes they are tired, some are singing, while others are oddly too animated. He may find in his fury that he will have lost one batch or more without being able to remedy it. He should closely watch matters of such importance. If the *banqueiro* or the assistant *banqueiro* lacks the intelligence or experience to supervise in his absence, he should not rely on them. Let him teach, advise, and if necessary reprimand them, making it plain to them the harm which the planter and the tenants will suffer if the sugarcane juice is lost in the cauldrons or if it goes improperly prepared into the molds.

He must ensure that the overseer of the mill regulates the crushing in such a way that more juice is not added to the vat than it can handle. It must be emptied before the juice begins to sour; refining, boiling, and stirring it when necessary.

Before he adds the ashes for refining into the boiling cauldrons, he tests the sugarcane liquid to see how it is, and subsequently see how the cauldrons pour it out and when they should be stopped. He should not allow the sugarcane liquid to congeal until he has ensured that the hot liquid is purified, as it should be. The same can be said for each transference from one cauldron to another, when it has to be cooked and stirred. The secret of success is the close attention to detail.

Both truth and justice oblige him not to mix the sugar of one tenant with that of another. For this reason, when he orders the molds to be placed in the cooling shed, he should see that they have marks so that they can be identified from each other, so that "mine" and "yours," the enemies of peace, should not be the cause of disputes. In order that his task may be perfectly done, he must keep in close touch with the mill overseer who sends him the boiling juice, with the *banqueiro* and the assistant *banqueiro*, who take over his duties at night, and with the sugar refiner, so that they may all observe the beginning of the sugar extraction process, done well or poorly, and the liquid poured into the molds. Let them be in unison, just as eyes that watch and hands that work together.

What is said above likewise applies largely to the *banqueiro*, who is the assistant to the sugar master, and to his helper, the assistant *banqueiro*. Besides this, these two officials also have to supervise the cooling shed, plug the holes in the sugar molds, have diggers make trenches for the discarded sugarcane stocks, make repairs, and empty the sugar made after its three stages of tempering, which will be explained later. After three days, the molds must be sent to the refinery either in wheelbarrows or on the shoulders of *negros*, where the refiner will take charge of them.

They must also try to make a just distribution of *claros*[20] among the slaves, as the planter orders, and ensure that the refinery is kept clean, with plenty of light, water, leaching ash, and all the tools they use there. It is the master's responsibility to see that, before the mill begins operation, none of the cauldrons or kettles need repairing, and whether their supports need rewiring or strengthening.

The salary of a sugar master in the mills that make four or five thousand loaves of sugar is about 130 *milréis*, particularly if he also oversees the refinery. On other, smaller plantations he receives only 100 *milréis*. The *banqueiro* receives 40 *milréis* on larger plantations, and 30 *milréis* on smaller ones. If the assistant *banqueiro* (who is usually a mulatto or Creole household slave) has performed his tasks satisfactorily, he is given some gift at the end of the harvest. The desire for this modest reward will give him some gentle encouragement for his work.

CHAPTER VII

The Sugar Refiner

I T IS THE RESPONSIBILITY of the sugar refiner to inspect the clay brought to the drying table to be dried over the ash-pan and to see if it is of the right kind, as will be explained later. He must also keep an eye on the person kneading to ensure he is handling the clay[21] in the right way, with the long stick and the mixing board. He must press the loaves into the molds and take them out. He must know when the sugar has dried and when the time has come to put on the first coating of clay. He must know how far this should cover it, and for how long it should be left before placing the second. He should also know how and when it should be moistened or washed, and how often. He should know what the indications are that the sugar has been refined properly or not, according to its different qualities and its thickness. He is also responsible for dealing with the molds of *mel*,[22] collecting the *mel*, cooking it, and mixing different lots or keeping them to make rum. He must make every effort to see that the collection vats for liquid sugars are kept clean. He must also try to get rid of the bats that are a common plague in nearly all the refineries.

A refiner on a plantation producing four thousand loaves of sugar gets a salary of fifty *milréis*. Those who have less work also receive less, in matching proportion.

CHAPTER VIII

The Bookkeeper on the Plantation

THIS CHAPTER DOES NOT apply to the bookkeeper in the city. His responsibilities are limited to receiving the sugar already packed, sending it to the warehouse, selling it, or shipping it, according to the planter's instructions. He has a double entry ledger. He keeps the accounts and acts as agent, accountant, attorney, and trustee for his patron. If he is hard worked he is paid a salary of forty or fifty *milréis*. Here I am speaking more particularly of the bookkeeper responsible for packing the sugar after it has been refined. It is his responsibility to order the removal of the sugar from the molds when it has already been refined and dried on clear and sunny days. He must be present when the white sugar is separated from the brown, and when it is dried in the drying room, dividing it and breaking it up, as will be explained later. It is he who weighs the sugar and who honestly divides it between the tenants and the planter. He deducts the tithe that is due to God, and the twentieth or fifth paid by those who cultivate their crops on land belonging to the mill. This is done in accordance with the agreements made in the leases and the usual local customs, which vary from place to place. He takes note of everything in order to later give an exact account. It is likewise his responsibility to have the chests raised and strengthened at the corners. He must also have the sugar packed and pounded, and grade it into the pure white, second quality,[23] and the brown sugar. He also makes the cases and the bundles when the owners of the sugar ask him to do so. Finally, he must have the chests nailed up and marked and keep the surplus sugar for the owners in a safe and dry place, as well as store the implements used. When the time for shipping the chests comes, he will hand them to the collecting agent, the owner, or to whomever was given a court order to impound them. This often happens because creditors often impound the sugar of the debtors before it leaves the mill. He must also ask for a receipt and an explanation of everything, so that he can give an account of it himself if anyone asks.

The salary of the bookkeeper on one of the larger plantations is about forty *milréis*, and if he does some supervisory work for some part of the day or night he gets fifty *milréis*. On the smaller plantations he is paid thirty *milréis*.

CHAPTER IX

How the Planter Should Treat His Slaves

T HE SLAVES ARE THE hands and the feet of the planter, for without them it is impossible in Brazil to create, maintain, and develop a plantation, or to have a productive mill. Whether the slaves turn out to be good or bad for the work depends on how the planter treats them. For this reason it is necessary to buy some slaves each year and to spread them out in the sugar fields, the allotments, the saw mills, and the boats. Since they are usually from different nations, and some are more ignorant than others, and their physique differs greatly, this distribution must be made carefully and intelligently, and not haphazardly. Those who come to Brazil are Ardas,[24] Minas,[25] Congolese, from São Tomé, from Angola, and from Cape Verde. Some are brought from Mozambique in the homeward-bound East Indiamen. Those from Ardas and Minas are the strongest, while those from Cape Verde and São Tomé are the weakest. Those from Angola who have been brought up in Luanda are better fitted to become skilled craftsmen than those from the other regions I have mentioned. Some of the Congolese are also fairly good and industrious, not only for work in the cane fields, but in the workshops and in household management.

Some of them arrive in Brazil very uncouth and sullen, and so they remain for the rest of their lives. Others become fluent in Portuguese in a few years and are clever, both regarding their ability to learn the catechism as well as in seeking a livelihood. These can be entrusted with a boat, or to deliver a message, or do anything they might normally be told to do. The women use the sickle and the hoe like men, but only the male slaves can use axes in the woods. From among the Portuguese-speaking slaves are chosen the boilers, carpenters, skimmers, boatmen, and sailors, since these jobs need greater expertise. Those who are placed on an estate when very young should not be moved from it against their will, for otherwise they mope and die. Those who are born in Brazil, or who are brought up in white households, give a good account of themselves if they take a liking to their masters. If they are well treated, any one of them is worth four raw hands.

Still better for any function are the mulattoes; but many of them, abusing the favors of their masters, are proud, vicious, and pride themselves on being ruffians, ready to commit any outrage. They, both male and female, are usually luckier than anyone else in Brazil. For, thanks to that portion of white blood in their veins—which is perhaps derived from their own masters, they bewitch these to such an extent that some masters will put up with anything from them, and forgive them any excess. It would seem as if their owners not only dare not scold them, but also deny them nothing. It is not easy to decide whether masters or mistresses are more blameworthy in this matter. For among both of them alike can be found persons who let themselves be ruled by mulattoes who are none of the best, thus verifying the proverb that says that "Brazil is Hell for *Negros,* Purgatory for Whites, and Paradise for Mulattoes," both male and female. Save only when on account of some suspicion, or jealousy, this love changes into hate and becomes armed with every sort of cruelty and rigor. It is a good thing to profit from their abilities when they are prepared to make good use of them, as some indeed do. But they should not be indulged so far that being given an inch they take a mile, and from being slaves they become masters. To emancipate unruly female mulattoes leads straight to perdition. The gold buying their freedom rarely comes from mines other than their own bodies by way of reoccurring sins. After they are freed, they continue to be the ruin of many.

Some planters do not like their slaves (of either sex) to live in lawful wedlock. Not only are they indifferent to their living together in an unmarried union, but they virtually encourage and initiate it. They say, "You, so and so, in due time will marry with so and so," and thenceforward they let them live together as if they were really man and wife. The planters excuse themselves by saying that they do not legally marry the slaves because if they got tired of being married they would kill themselves quickly with poison or through witchcraft. These means are not lacking among the slaves, who are noted practitioners of diabolical arts. Other masters, after the slaves have been married for some time, separate them for years on end just as if they were single, which cannot be done in good conscience. Others are so negligent regarding the salvation of their slaves that they do not have them baptized for a long time while they work in the cane fields or the mill. Many of those who are baptized do not know who their creator is, what they ought to believe, and what law they ought to keep. Nor do they know how to pray to God, why Christians go to church, why they worship the consecrated Host, or what they ought to say to the priest when they kneel down and whisper in his ear. They also do not know whether they have a soul and whether it dies, and where it goes when it leaves the body. The most ignorant newcomers quickly learn who their master is and his name, how many holes of cassava they must dig each day, how many stands of cane they have to cut, how many loads of firewood they have to deliver, and other things belonging to their master's normal service. They likewise know how to ask his forgiveness when they have done wrong and persuade him not to punish them by promising to behave better. Yet, in spite of all this, there are planters who maintain that these people cannot learn how to make confession, or how to beg God for forgiveness, nor pray with their rosary beads, nor learn the Ten Commandments! This is merely for want of teaching, and because the planters do not consider the lengthy account they must one day render to God, for as Saint Paul says, Christians who neglect their slaves are behaving worse than unbelievers who do so. Nor do such planters compel them to hear Mass on Holy Days, but on the contrary they keep them so busy that they have no time for it. Nor do they ask the chaplain to catechize them, paying him a larger stipend for his work if need be.

It is obvious that the slaves should not be denied adequate feeding and clothing, and should not be overworked. For the owner rightfully ought to give whoever serves him sufficient food, medicines when sick, and the wherewithal to dress himself decently, as befits the servile state, and not let him appear nearly naked in the streets. The owner should also regulate the work in such a way that it is not more than his laborers can perform, if he wishes them to last. It is customary to say in Brazil that the three p's are necessary for the slave—namely, *pao* [stick], *pão* [bread], and *panno* [cloth]. Although they begin badly by placing the stick—the punishment—first, yet would to God that the feeding and clothing were as equally plentiful as the punishment often is. This castigation is often inflicted for a doubtful or fanciful reason, and with very cruel means (even when the crimes are undeniable), which would not be used on a brute beast. Some owners pay more attention to a horse than to half a dozen slaves. Their horse has attendants and someone to cut grass for him and is wiped down when in a sweat, and his saddle and bridle are decorated with gold.

Still greater care should be taken with new slaves for they have as yet no means of livelihood, as have those who are engaged in cultivating their allotments. Those who have them, thanks to their own industry, should not be remembered as slaves when the work is being apportioned but then forgotten when they need medicine and clothing. They should be granted time off on Sundays and Holy Days. When their owner does not allow this but makes them work as on ordinary weekdays, they sulk and curse him sullenly. Some planters give their slaves one day a week in which to cultivate their allotments, sometimes sending the overseer with them to see that they do so. This suffices to prevent them from going hungry, and besieging the planter's house each day, begging for a ration of cassava flour. On the other hand, if they are not given any cassava, nor time to cultivate it, and if they are expected at the mill from sunrise to sundown, how can this pass unpunished in the Tribunal of God? If the refusal of alms to someone who begs from sheer necessity is to refuse alms to Christ Our Lord, as He says in the Gospel, what of the owner who refuses to give food and clothing to his slave? And he who gives fine stuffs, silk, and other adornments to those women who are the cause of his ruin, how will he justify himself if he subsequently refuses to give four or five lengths of cotton and a few pieces of coarse cloth to the slave who is bathed in sweat working for him, and who hardly has time to find a root and a crab to eat? And if, in addition to all this, the punishments are excessive and oft repeated, the slaves will both desert and flee to the bush, or else they will commit suicide, as they do by suffocating or hanging themselves. They may try to kill those who treat them so badly, through witchcraft or the black arts if need be. Or else they will cry so loud to God that He will hear them, and do to the planter what He did to the Egyptians when they oppressed the Hebrews beyond endurance, by inflicting terrible plagues upon their estates and children, as may be read in the Holy Scripture. Or, just as the Hebrews were carried captive to Babylon as a punishment for the harsh treatment they gave their slaves, so He may allow some cruel enemy to carry away these planters from their lands, so that they may experience therein what a painful life they gave and continually give to their slaves.

Not to punish the excesses that the slaves commit would be an inexcusable fault. However, these crimes must be investigated carefully first, so as to avoid punishing the innocent. The planter must hear the accused, and if he finds him guilty, punish him with a moderate flogging, or by putting him in the chain gang or in the dungeon for some time. The planter should not punish at the spur of the moment, with a vengeful mind, with his own hand, and with instruments of torture, or perchance inflicting burns with a flame or molten wax, or branding the face. These things cannot be tolerated from barbarians, still less among Catholic Christians. It is certain that if the planter treats the slaves like a father, giving them what they need to sustain and clothe themselves and some needful respite from work, he can subsequently treat them like a master. They will not then object to being punished rightly but mercifully for the misdeeds they have committed. If after they have shown their weaknesses by committing these offenses, they come forward voluntarily to beg pardon of their masters, or if they find someone to accompany them, then it is the custom in Brazil to pardon them. They should know that such is the case, for otherwise they may all flee to some community of runaways in the bush.[26] If they are captured, they might kill themselves before the planter has time to whip them, or perhaps one of their relatives will become the avenger, either through witchcraft or poison.

Slaves should not be completely forbidden from enjoying their traditional pastimes, which are their only solace in captivity. Otherwise, they will become miserable, melancholy, unhealthy, and disheartened. For this reason, the planter should not object to the slaves crowning their kings, singing, and dancing respectably on some days in the year. Nor should he object to their enjoying themselves innocently in the evenings after morning celebrations of their feast days of Our Lady of the Rosary, Saint Benedict, and of the patron saint of the plantation chapel. These celebrations should be at no cost to the slaves. The planter should liberally give to the judges of their festivities and bestow some reward for their continual toil. If the male and female judges of the feast have to spend their own money, this will be the cause of many offenses and insults to God. There are few of them who can lawfully save enough money for these festivals.

One thing that must be avoided on the plantation is the slaves getting drunk on fermented sugarcane wine,[27] or on rum. It will be enough to allow them some sweet wine, which is harmless, and with which they can barter for flour, beans, sweet cassava, and potatoes.

It is a good thing if the planters take care sometimes to give surplus goods to the little *negro* children, for this makes the slaves serve them willingly and multiply new male and female slaves. On the other hand, some female slaves deliberately try to abort their pregnancies on the plantations where they are ill treated, so that the children inside them will not suffer as they have.

How the Planter Should Act in Directing His Family and Ordinary Household Expenses

S INCE THE STRUCTURE of a plantation demands such vast expenses as we have explained above, it can easily be seen how much economy is necessary in managing the household. More good horses than are necessary, fancy musicians, trumpeters, instrumentalists, and pampered lackeys do not help to increase wealth but only to diminish it with debts and mortgages. Still less useful are continual amusements and superfluous banquets, the festive clothes, the elaborate sedan chairs, and gambling. By these paths, in a few years some wealthy planters find themselves reduced to the status of poor and miserable tenants, unable to find dowries for their daughters or any honest means to assist their sons.

It is bad to be called a penny-pincher, but it is no praiseworthy thing to be called a spendthrift. He who is resolved to lead a planter's laborious life must retire from the city and escape the civic duties that would distract him. On the other hand, he could maintain two homes, with double expenses, and with marked detriment to the one from which he is unavoidably absent. If he keeps his sons always with him on the plantation, they are liable to grow up as country bumpkins. They will have no subjects of conversation in society other than dogs, horses, and oxen. If they are left alone in the city, this gives them the freedom to court vice and contract shameful diseases that cannot be cured easily. In order, therefore, to avoid these two extremes, the best thing to do is to put them in the house of some honorable and respectable relative or friend where they will not have the opportunity of being led astray. This guardian will be glad to keep an eye on them, and give completely reliable information about their good or poor behavior, and their progress or negligence in study. The planter should not allow his wife to send them money or to secretly order his bookkeeper or agent in the city to do so. Nor should he always believe that when they ask for money to buy books, it might not also be for gambling. For this reason, he should instruct the attorney or the merchant who acts as his agent not to give them anything without his order. They will be very clever in inventing all sorts of specious pretexts and convincing reasons when asking for money. This is especially true when they are already following a course of study and want to enjoy a good life for three years at the expense of their father or uncle, who remains on his estate and does not know what is happening in the city. When these fathers or uncles boast in conversation of having an Aristotle in the lecture room, it may well be that they have an Asínio or an Aprício in the market place.[28] However, the planter may decide to keep his sons at home on the plantation, and be satisfied with their learning reading, writing, and arithmetic, and gathering some notions of history and current affairs. This will allow them to converse in society. If he does this, the father should not neglect to watch them closely as they grow older. The open countryside is likewise a place of great freedom that nonetheless contains rocks and thorns. If oxen and horses are fenced in so that they cannot stray beyond the pasture, what is wrong in placing some restrictions on the sons, whether inside or outside the house? Experience shows this to be necessary. This is good as long as the father's circumspection is prudent and not overly strict, which may encourage malice. The best example, however, is the good behavior of the parents. The surest way of obtaining peace of mind is to marry off both daughters and sons at the proper time. If the parents will be contented with equal marriages, there is no shortage of families with whom they can make suitable exchanges and receive benefits in return.

CHAPTER XI

How the Planter Should Receive Guests,
Whether Religious or Laymen

Hospitality is both an act of courtesy and a Christian duty, and it is much exercised and highly esteemed in Brazil. Since there are no inns outside the cities, all wayfarers must resort to the plantations, where they usually find free of charge what would cost money in other lands. This applies both to the numerous religious figures, who go about seeking alms, and to the missionaries who work in the Bay of Bahia and in the hinterland. They exercise their sacred ministry to the great benefit of souls. This also applies to laymen who, either from necessity or because they are friends or relatives, seek hospitality on their travels.

It is a good thing to have a separate house for the guests, because it is then easier to accommodate them without inconveniencing the household. Having a separate house will also avoid infringing the privacy of the interior rooms, where the wives, daughters, and serving maids are busy preparing dinner and supper.

Guests should not be treated more lavishly than their respective ranks demand, since a large number have to be entertained in the course of the year. Chickens and pigs, or some fish from the sea or from the river, together with some shellfish from the mangrove swamps and what the mill provides in the way of sugar and sweets — this is enough to prevent anybody from complaining with reason. To go further than this (save in special cases for justifiable causes) is to exceed the limits of hospitality and will impoverish the planter to such an extent that he cannot be equally generous in the future.

To give alms is to lend money at interest to God, who will repay it a hundredfold. But first of all, one should pay what is due to the government, and then piously give alms as far as one's capital and yearly income will allow. In this connection the planter will never have reason to regret being an alms-giver, and the sons will learn to imitate their father. If he leaves them inclined to works of charity, he will leave them very rich and with their wealth secure.

For vagrants, let him have hoes and sickles ready. If they wish to stay on the plantation he can tell them through the overseer that if they will work they will be paid their daily wage. In this way, they will either continue on their journey or else become day laborers instead of vagrants.

It is likewise not convenient that the sugar master, the bookkeeper, or the overseer should host prominent people from the city or elsewhere for any length of time in their houses, where they will pass their time in idleness. This is especially true if they are young and unmarried men. These guests only serve to distract the skilled workers from their respective duties. These guests would also rouse the female slaves on the plantation. They are easily led into evil ways through their immoderate desires. The employees should be cautioned about this when they are engaged, as otherwise they will find themselves saddled with nephews or cousins whose vices cause them sorrow and displeasure.

The missionaries who unselfishly go about doing their work should be received with a right good will. If they meet with a cold reception, they might think that the planter, either through little love of God, miserliness, or some other reason, does not approve of missionary work. This work is important because consciences are adjusted with God, instruction is given to the ignorant, long-standing feuds and scandals are ended, and all are exhorted to think of the salvation of their souls.

How the Planter Should Deal with Merchants as Well as with His Agents in the Market Place; Some of the Ways of Buying and Selling Sugar, as Practiced in Brazil

THE CREDIT OF A PLANTER depends on his reliability; that is to say, on the punctuality and loyalty with which he keeps his promises. Tenants should be able to depend upon this, as he decides the days they are to press their cane and receive their share of the sugar. This reliability extends to the employees in the payment of their salaries, those who supply the firewood for the ovens, timber for the mill, tiles and molds for the boiling house, boards for chests, as well as oxen and horses for running the estate. His reliability will gain him the confidence of merchants and his agents in the market place, those who advance him money to buy slaves, copper, iron, steel, rigging, pitch, and sails, and other supplies on trust. If at the time of the fleet's departure, the planters do not pay what they owe, they will not be able to receive any supplies for the next harvest. They will also be unable to find anyone willing to entrust money or goods to the hands of debtors who either do not pay at all, or else pay so slowly and laboriously that the creditor is menaced with bankruptcy.

There are some years in which, owing to heavy mortality among the slaves, horses, oxen, or to the small yield from the cane, the planters cannot possibly pay all that they had promised. However, if they do not try to repay even a fraction of what they owe, then they do not deserve to be granted the respite for which they ask. This is particularly true when it is known that they spent money on riotous living and gambling, rather than saving to repay their creditors.

In other years, when the yield is adequate and there are few or no losses, there is no reason to disappoint the merchants or agents who represent the larger commercial barons and to whom they have to render an account. Therefore, it is not very surprising if, after the contract has not been honored for some time and they are faced with the prospect of no profit, but on the contrary increasing loss, they moderately raise the prices of goods sold on credit. God knows when they will be able to collect the payment.

To buy the sugar in advance at the rate of two *cruzados*, for example, which is commonly worth twelve or more *tostões*[29] at harvest time, has its drawbacks. The buyer is certain of his profit and the seller is morally certain to lose. This is especially true when the man who advances the money does not need to purchase anything else before the time comes to ship the sugar to Portugal.

Whoever buys or sells sugar in advance at the price it will be worth at the time of the fleet's landing makes a legitimate contract. Both buyer and seller are taking an equal risk. This assumes the price will be at the prevailing market rate for sugar at that time and not privately arranged. The seller may need to do this because he is forced by necessity to sell.

To buy on installment means to pay down forthwith a part of the price and to pay the rest later in quarterly or annual installments, according to the contract, until the whole is paid off. It is legitimate to add a penalty of a stipulated number of additional *cruzados* if any installment falls behind. However, no claims can be made for the payment of interest on money already repaid, since interest is only paid for the principal.

The expression "selling the sugar captive" means selling it with the responsibility on the buyer of paying all expenses, excepting only the three *tostões* which are paid in Bahia, for that is a charge on the shipper.

To sell the sugar "free" at the rate of ten *tostões* for each *arroba*,[30] for example, means that the buyer has to pay the seller at the rate of ten *tostões* for each *arroba* and has to pay all the expenses himself.

Whoever buys the sugar "captive" and ships it, can afterward sell it "free" and the next buyer pays the subsequent costs.

To buy the sugar by "heads" means to buy the chests of sugar at the number of *arrobas* by which they are marked, with a deduction of half an *arroba* for breakage.

When a chest of sugar is weighed for the purpose of paying duty, if the person weighing does so favorably he says, for example, that a chest of thirty *arrobas* weighs only twenty-eight, and the Crown lets this go as a favor. However, that chest is not sold at this weight, but at its true weight, which is ascertained when it is weighed on the scales outside the Customs House, which are there in order to settle any doubts.

It is a lawful and just contract to sell lands for less than they are worth on condition that the cane planted on them must be pressed in the seller's mill.

It is a common practice in Brazil for a planter to buy, from a tenant farmer who is free to press his cane anywhere, the obligation to have it crushed in his mill for as long as the tenant does not refund the sum of money advanced him for assuming this obligation. The lawyers defend this as a lawful contract because this is not money loaned him in return for pressing the cane. It is the outright purchase of the obligation to have the cane pressed in the planter's mill so that the planter can get half of it. The door is always open for the tenant to escape this obligation at any time, simply by repaying the planter the money he originally received from him.

[BOOK TWO]

CHAPTER I

The Choice of Land on Which to Plant the Cane, and for Supplying Provisions Needed for the Mill

WHETHER THE LANDS are good or bad determines if a royal mill will yield a profit or a loss. Those lands which are called *massapés*—black, thick earth—are the best for planting cane. Next come the *saloens:* red earth capable of only a few years of cuttings, for it is soon exhausted. The *areiscas,* which are a mixture of sand and *saloens,* are useful for growing cassava and vegetables, but not for cane. I would say the same about the white earth called Lands of Sand, like those of Camamú[1] and of Saubâra.[2]

The land chosen for pasture around the mill must have water and must be fenced, either with live plants, such as pines, or with stockades and rods cut from the bush. The best pasture has a lot of grass, partly on the high ground and partly on the low ground. In this way, at all times of the year, the oxen and the other beasts will find something to eat, either in the one part or in the other. The pasture must be kept clear of all the other plants that kill the grass. In the winter, the pigs must be kept out of it because otherwise they root it all up. There should be one or two stockyards in it where the oxen can be put to eat the sprouts of the cane, and to be on hand to use with the carts. Likewise the other beasts should be in their respective runs, so that it will not be necessary to search high and low for them.

Besides mares and oxen, the sheep and the goats should also be kept in the pastures. The smaller animals, such as turkeys, hens, and ducks, should be kept around the mill, as they are the easiest to slaughter for meals for unexpected guests. Since sheep and horses graze very close to the roots of the grass, they are prejudicial to the pasture of the oxen. For this reason it would be better for them to be pastured separately, if possible.

The woods will supply the timber and the firewood for the ovens. The marshy ground in which mangrove trees grow will yield timbers for roofs and shellfish. The *apicus*[3] will yield the clay to refine the sugar in the molds and for the pottery. In the opinion of some people, the manufacture of pottery cannot be omitted from the royal mills.

A royal mill needs all these different kinds of lands. Some serve for cane, others for growing food for the people, and others for the building and equipment of the mill, apart from the materials imported from the Kingdom of Portugal. However, not all the mills can enjoy such good fortune; on the contrary, there is not one lacking some of these things. Those situated by the seashore usually lack sufficient allotments of land and need firewood. Those farther inland lack many other useful things that plantations in the *Recôncavo*[4] by the seaside usually possess. All in all, it depends on whether the plantation owner has or lacks capital, people, faithful and experienced employees, oxen and animals, boats and carts, whether his plantation is well or poorly managed. If he does not have people to work and cultivate the lands at the proper time, then this will be the same as owning an uncleared forest with little or no profit. Just as in civilized life, it is not enough to have a good nature if one does not have a master who, with his instruction, helps one to improve.

CHAPTER II

Planting and Weeding Canes, and the Different Kinds of Them

W HEN THE BEST LAND has been chosen for the cane, it is cleared, burned, weeded, and cleared of anything in the way. It is then plowed in furrows, one and a half *palmas*[5] deep and two broad, with a ridge between each furrow, so that the cane should not be smothered as it grows. In these furrows, either the cane is planted in shoots or the canes are planted in stocks measuring three or four *palmas*. If it is a small type of cane, then it is planted whole, one near the other, pushing it in with the foot. They are then covered over lightly with earth. After a few days, the shoots begin to grow and gradually reveal their greenery at ground level, taking root easily and growing more or less, according to the quality of the soil and the clemency or inclemency of the weather. But if they are planted too close together, or if when being weeded the earth gets too close to them, then they cannot sprout as they should.

The planting of the cane in the higher lands of Bahia begins after the first rains at the end of February or at the beginning of March, and continues until the end of May. On the lowlands and the flat lands (which are fresher and more humid), the planting is also done in the months of July and August, and for a few days in September. Any kind of cane which is not dried out or damaged, or which has very small stalks, is good for planting. If the soil is new and strong, this causes the cane to grow very luxuriantly and it is called "wild cane." The first and second times that it is cut, it does not usually yield good sugar, since it is very watery. However, after the soil has let loose its energy, even though the cane grows extraordinarily, it yields as well as it looks in appearance. One sometimes finds these kinds of canes seven, eight, or nine *palmas* high, and they look as outstanding in the fields as captains do in armies.

The best cane has broad and clean joints. Canes with small and hairy joints are the worst. Narrow joints are caused by drought or by cold, because both of these contract them. If they are hairy, they have not been weeded in due time. The cane should be weeded as soon as there are any weeds or grass to remove. In the winter the grass that is removed soon grows again, so that the most important cleanings are the first ones, made to allow the cane to grow and prevent it from being smothered by the wild grass. For after it has grown, it is easier for it to resist the smaller weeds. Thus we see that the earliest vices are those that spoil good character. The canes planted on the hillsides are normally cleaner than those planted on the flat lands. Just as water running down the hillsides in the rainy season prevents the weeds from easily growing there, it also creates stagnant pools in the flat lands. This makes these lands always very damp and consequently very propitious for a renewed growth of the wild grass.

For this reason, in some soils weeding three times is not enough. In others, the farmer can rest after the second weeding, according to the seasons being more or less rainy. Just as there are children so docile that they behave themselves after the first reprimand, there are others who do not improve in spite of repeated punishments.

Likewise the ratoons[6] (shoots from the stumps of the canes which have been cut in due time, or burned for being too old, or because the canes fell down in such ways that they could not be cut, or through some natural disaster) serve for planting. If they are not killed by severe cold or great drought, and earth is put round them, they sprout again. In this way, the shoots of cane can be renewed for five or six years or more. So useful is human ingenuity in deriving advantage even from what seems useless and not worth further attention! It is true that when the soil becomes exhausted, the ratoon likewise loses its vigor. After six or seven years, the cane decays and easily becomes withered until it is quite dry and distressed. For this reason, one should not demand more from the soil and from the ratoon than they are able to give, particularly if they are not helped in some way. The wisdom of the farmer consists in his planting the cane successively, so that when the old cane is cut for milling, the new is left standing for the next harvest. In this way it nurtures with its greenery the hope of the forthcoming yield, which is the reward of his continual labor. To plant a "task" of canes [a *tarefa*] is the same as planting a space of thirty square fathoms [*braças*] of land.[7] Finally, as the diversity of the soils and the climate demands different types of cultivation, it is necessary to learn from and to follow the advice of the old hands. They have learned much from time and experience. It is best to ask them concerning any doubts in order to be sure what you are doing is correct.

CHAPTER III

Enemies of the Cane in the Field

VARIATIONS IN THE weather are the principal enemy of the cane, as is also the case with other fruits and crops of the earth. With much reason, God armed the elements against us in punishment for our sins. Perhaps it was so we would learn patience, or that we would remember that He is the author and the preserver of all things, and that we should have recourse to Him in such crises.

The fields on the hillsides are better able to resist successive rains, but they are the first to suffer from drought. On the other hand, the flat lands do not respond so quickly to the force of excessive heat, but they suffer sooner from excessive rains. The cane of Bahia requires rain in the months of October, November, and December, and for the new plants in February. It also later needs the sun, which usually does not fail, just as the rains do not fail in those months. However, the most dangerous, continual, and most familiar enemy of the cane is the wild grass. It persecutes the cane more or less throughout its life. While the cane must be planted and cut at certain seasons, weeding it is a continual necessity that obliges the planter's slaves to go about always with a hoe in hand. Whenever any other occupation outside the cane fields is finished, then time is never wasted in ordering them to weed. This is an exercise that should be a constant with those who bring up their children properly and take care to cultivate the soul. Even though this enemy, the wild grass, suffices for many, there is no lack of equally troublesome and dangerous others. As soon as the cane begins to sprout above the earth, the goats immediately try to attack it. The oxen and the horses begin by eating the shoots, and they afterward tear down and trample the cane. The rats and the pigs root it out. Thieves steal it in sheaves, and no lad or wayfarer passes by who does not want to eat and toy with it, at the cost of whoever planted it. Although the farmers resign themselves somehow to enduring the petty thefts of the fruits of their labor, they are sometimes compelled in a righteous anger to kill pigs, goats, and oxen that their owners did not trouble to keep in fenced pastures or more distant places. This was even when they have been begged to do so and warned to put a stop to this damage. This in turn gives way to complaints, enmities, and hatreds, which end in deaths or with bloody and insulting deeds of vengeance. For this reason, everyone should try to protect his own cane fields and avoid giving others any cause for making justifiable complaints against his own carelessness. Everyone should reckon the harm done to others by the resentment he would feel for his own losses.

CHAPTER IV

Cutting the Cane and Carrying It to the Mill

WHEN THE MILL BEGINS operation (which in the *Recôncavo* of Bahia usually is in August), this is also the time when the sickle should cut the ripe cane. The cane is best left before cutting for seventeen or eighteen months in the ground. After that, unless it is oppressed by a great drought, it may be safely left in the same ground for another seven or eight months. As soon as it is finally ready, the order should be given to cut it, after previously fixing the day on which the milling should begin. This will avoid its becoming tainted in the mill, or too dry when exposed to the sun in the harbor,[8] if this is distant from the mill. The tenant farmer who brings his cane to the mill first should be informed so that he can press his share. On the other hand, the lazy one who misses his turn on the appointed day by failing to turn up should lose his place. It is the mill owner who allots the days for pressing his own cane and that of the farmers. Each is accorded his turn and advised in a timely manner by the mill supervisor.

Twelve to eighteen pairs of slaves with sickles work in the field to cut the cane, depending if the stocks are large or small. The amount of cane that is sent for pressing at any one time is called a "task." It is the equivalent of twenty-four cart loads of cane, each cart being the standard measurement of eight *palmas* high and seven broad, capable of containing a greater or smaller number of sheaves of cane, depending on whether the cane is large or small. Fewer sheaves of large cane are needed to make up a task, whereas more are needed if the cane is small. Smaller sheaves occupy less space, both in the cart and the barge. Larger sheaves take up more space, since they are both longer and thicker. However, there are very few carts that can carry more than 150 sheaves of cane. Owners of the cane fields know very well from previous harvests exactly how many tasks their cane fields contain.

The first cane that should be cut is the old, which cannot wait any longer. It is unlike death, whose sickle cuts down indifferently young and old. This cane must be cut at a time when it does no damage to the ratoon, depending on whether the soils are more or less cold and the days are more or less hot and dry. This is the reason why, on some lands, the cane cannot be cut until after the end of February, and on others it can still be cut in March and April. In regard to cutting the new cane, if the farmer is very ambitious and eager to make a lot of sugar, he will cut it all in one harvest. He will then find himself with little or none in the next. For this reason, care should be taken in cutting the new cane with an eye toward the future. The planter should plan according to the amount already planted, on the basis of well-considered and reliable calculations. This is what sensible prudence and economy dictate in any other work or business.

Both the male and the female slaves are employed in cutting the cane, but as a rule the males do the cutting and the females tie up the sheaves. A sheaf consists of twelve canes. Each male slave has the task of cutting in one day seven "hands" of ten sheaves for each one of the "fingers," making altogether 350 bundles.[9] The female slave has to bundle as many with the cut tops of the same canes. If they have any time left over, they can spend it whatever way they please. This favor is not allowed when they are engaged in weeding the cane, for this work lasts from sunrise to sunset. Also, they do not enjoy this favor in any other labor not allotted them on the basis of a task. The reason the task is counted by "fingers" and "hands," as noted above, is to make allowance for the ignorance of raw slaves, who would not otherwise understand and cannot count properly.

The actual cutting is done as follows. The slave grasps with his left hand as many canes as he can secure. With the sickle in his right hand, he strips the outer leaves, which afterward are burned. This work is done either at dawn or at night or when the wind drops and offers an opportunity. The ash serves to fertilize the soil. He then lifts his left hand higher up and cuts off the tops of the stalks with the sickle, and these are given to the oxen to eat. Finally sliding his left hand down the cane he cuts it close to the ground. The closer the sickle is to the earth, the better. Whoever follows the cutter (and the follower is usually a female slave) then bundles up the clean canes in sheaves of dozen each, as stated above, tying them up with the tops of the stalks. The sheaves thus tied are carried in carts to the port, or if the mill lies inland, the cart takes them to it.

Carts transport the cane by land, and each plantation ought to have two of them, or more if it is a large plantation. If transported by sea, they go in two barges without sails, rowed by four sweeps instead of oars. These are powered by as many *negro* boatmen and the headman, who acts as helmsman. For this purpose, two large barges are required, like those they call *rodeiras*.[10] The farmer has the responsibility of cutting the cane and transporting it at his cost to the port where the mill owner's barge receives it and carries it free of charge by sea to the mill. The farmer's slaves load it in the barge, and the boatmen then arrange it. But if the mill lies inland, the cost of transportation to the mill is paid by the owner of the cane, regardless of whether he brings the cane voluntarily to the mill or whether he is under contract to do so.

Transporting the cane by land during the rainy and muddy season will involve the death of many oxen. This is particularly true if they have just been brought from elsewhere and arrive thin and weak and they have not become accustomed to the new pasture and work. This is still more so in regard to the transportation of the crates of sugar, as will be explained below. For this reason, when the oxen arrive from the interior, weak and exhausted from the long trail, it is best not to yoke them in the carts until after they have been at least a year and a half in the new pasture. They will gradually become accustomed to light work, and this should begin in the summer and not in the winter. Otherwise, it may well happen, as it did a few years ago, when one mill alone lost 211 oxen: some in the mud, some at the mill, and some in the pasture. When the pressing is done by waterpower and barges are used for the transportation of the cane, the mill must have four or five carts, with twelve or fourteen yokes of very strong oxen. How many more will a mill need if the milling is done with cattle and oxen, and it has its own cane that must be brought from afar to the mill? Great attention should be paid to this point, so as to ensure that as many and as strong oxen as are necessary are bought at the right time. It is better to give eight *milréis* for one robust and domesticated ox than to give as much for two small and lean ones that lack the strength to endure the work.[11]

CHAPTER V

The Mill, the Building Housing It,
and How Water Powers It

EVEN THOUGH "MILL" is the name given to the entire complex of buildings, with workshops for milling the cane, cooking, and refining the sugar, all in all, it is the same to say "mill house" as "building for milling cane," which houses the ingeniously invented object. As we have now arrived at this structure with cane brought to the rollers, we will give some description of it and how the work there is conducted to press the sugar from the cane. This is based on what I saw at the royal mill of Sergipe do Conde, which is the best known of all the mills in Bahia.

The building rises at the edge of a river, with seventeen great brick pillars, four *palmas* wide and twenty-two high, spaced fifteen *palmas* from each other. It is a lofty and spacious structure, the roof covered with roofing tiles. These sit on straight beams, tied in place, from a type of wood called *lei*, which is the strongest wood in Brazil. No other place produces a wood of equal quality. The structure has two verandas around it, one for receiving cane and firewood and the other to store extra wood. This is what is called the milling house, capable of comfortably processing four tasks of cane without disrupting the flow of those who work there as well as those coming and going. There is ample space to keep the way open for other work areas, particularly for those just next to the furnaces and cauldrons. This entire structure is 193 *palmas* long and 86 wide. Such a special artifice of axles and wheels mills the cane here that it deserves special attention and a more complete description.

In order to power the rollers, a good deal of water is diverted upriver into an aqueduct where it flows behind a dam or into a tank lined with brick or tile. A channel conducts the water behind a dam or into a tank. In order to power the mill, water is released and allowed to run through

Simon de Vries, "Brasilise Suykerwerken," from *Curieuse aenmerckingen*, Utrecht, 1682 (JCB 03016-2). Courtesy of the John Carter Brown Library at Brown University

a large and well-lined channel falling at a slow incline. In this way, the water moves smoothly with greater impetus and force past a diverter that can deflect water if necessary, such as when heavy rains fall or when it rains more than usual. There is an opening for the water to enter two pipes, one that takes it to the cauldrons and the other to take it to cool the axis inside the large roller of the mill. This is connected by a board to another channel that conducts water to an open wooden pipe, called the *caliz*. It rests on brick pillars and its end is lowered, meeting the top of the water wheel. Since this water strikes the cavities of the wheel, this is called "the striker." It fills the cavities on the wheel with water and ensures its continued motion. The axles of this wheel, one on the outside and another on the inside of the mill, rest on two supports made of wood with bronze tops. These hold up two supports inside and two outside for the channel holding the axis. On top of these, as we have stated, there is always a little water trickling down to keep it cool, and prevent it from becoming overheated by constant use. The water keeps the heat in check.

The spokes of the large wheel support its curving shape. On the inside, the cavities made in the wheel to hold water are linked together by sheathing along the inside of the two edges of the wheel and held by many iron bolts with their washers and bolts covered so that the wheel and the cavities do not move when the water pours out and the wheel can make a secure turn. Near the outside wheel are two big, thick pillars with three beams also secured elsewhere. One of these supports the end of the water channel feeding the wheel, two support the tip of the feeding channel, and another controls the *pejador*,[12] or stop. The *pejador* consists of a plank, slightly wider than the wheel, ten or twelve *palmas* in length with its edges like those of a large tray, underneath the feeding channel, secured by a pin. It is possible to pull or move the pin with little or no resistance because the hole for the pin is large enough to allow this. A large iron spike is attached to the lower part of the *pejador* on the side adjoining the wall of the mill. It is also attached to an iron chain. The chain is attached to a support called the *mourão*, and these act just like hinges. Through a hole in this wall, using a hand or a handle, the *pejador* can be operated by those persons standing at the rollers to make the wheel stop or run as they wish, by pushing or pulling the *pejador*. When it covers the cavities on the wheel, this prevents the channel from providing the motion to make it move. By allowing the water to rush into the cavities, it will make the wheel turn, and when it does, so will the rollers. This is very necessary in the event an accident occurs and someone has to run for help, as well as to minimize danger. This plank is called the *pejador* because to stop the mill is called to *pejar*. Perhaps this term is used since when a royal mill is slowed down or impeded, even for a moment and not permanently, it is not milling or in movement. This stoppage begins at the exterior of the structure, where the movement begins.

Entering the milling house, the movement is transferred to the rollers as follows. One end of the axle of the large wheel projects outside the milling house; on the inside, it has the last piece, a fixed smaller wheel with pegs all around it. When this smaller wheel turns around the axle on its rotation, these pegs interlock with pegs of another large wheel, called the flywheel. It is called this because the way in which it rotates above the rollers is like a bird flying when the wheel makes

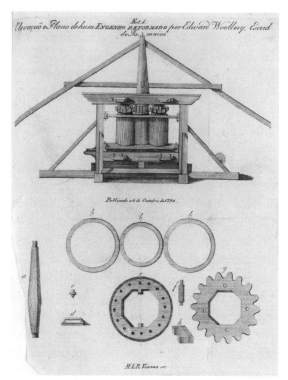

José Mariano da Conceiçao Velloso, "Elevaçao e
Plano de hum Engenho Reformado," Lisbon, 1798
(JCB 72-196-5). Courtesy of the John Carter
Brown Library at Brown University

its turns. The pegs on the smaller wheel that I saw numbered 32, and
the flywheel had 112. Since the spokes of the flywheel pass through
the middle roller, it is through these that torque is induced in the center roller. This roller, in turn, is surrounded by cogwheels and teeth
that interlock with those of the two smaller rollers on its sides. By this
method using cogwheels and teeth, the rollers all turn together.

The spokes on the flywheel are eight, four on top and four on the
bottom. The ones on the bottom have cross-beams as well, to provide
greater strength. The three rollers of the mill are round cylinders. The
smaller ones are five and a half *palmas* high, and the larger one in the
middle is six *palmas* high and has a greater circumference than the oth-

ers. It has to be the strongest of the three because the other two on its sides are constantly pressing against it, and it wears more than the others. For that reason, as a general rule the smaller rollers have nine teeth and the larger one has eleven, and this one (to use the language of the mill) has a high neck and head, in accordance with the height of the mill. Normally the roller is twelve *palmas* high. The top is two and a half *palmas* high and thinner than the neck. The top enters a hole in a piece of lumber called a *porca*,[13] held in place by two beams of forty-two *palmas* in length, supported by four braces sixteen *palmas* high and four wide. Their supports are proportionally spaced. Even though the two smaller rollers do not have necks, their iron axles enter a piece of lumber with holes in it, called *mesas* or *gatos,* which hold the rollers securely in place. The exterior of the three axles from the midpoint down are covered in iron plate fastened with nails. The tops of these are squared off and aligned so that the plating is even on all three rollers. Underneath the plating, the axles are encircled with layers of *lei* wood so that it will harden and become more capable of resisting the pressure it will encounter in milling. On top of the sheathing is a circle or band of wood that is actually part of the roller. It has the iron stripped away, and then immediately there is a band of teeth made from *lei* wood embedded in the roller between spaces (these are cavities or spaces between each of the teeth) that allow the two gears to mesh. The teeth from one roller enter and leave the spaces in the other roller. In order for this to work, the teeth and the spaces are exactly the same size. That is, the thickness and height of the teeth match the spaces in their width and depth. They are about six or seven fingers in width and the length of a hand and four or five fingers thick, almost flat and rounded on the edges. Even though between the teeth of the smaller rollers there are spaces that are carefully measured and equally spaced at one large *palma* each, those spaces on the larger roller are larger than a *palma* and are about the thickness of two *cruzado* coins. This is done to keep the two rollers turning correctly and to prevent the teeth from both rollers entering spaces in the other roller at the same time. One turns after the other, and in this manner the three turn the way they were designed. In order to ensure this, the teeth and the spaces of one roller do not meet the teeth and spaces of the other. That is, the teeth on the larger roller match the spaces on the smaller, and the teeth of the smaller fit the spaces on the larger roller. The teeth (as I have said) are on the exterior part of the roller and are a bit flat and rounded at the ends. They are four or five fingers in width and the thickness is the same. They penetrate another four fingers from their bases into the roller they meet. This secures them in place, as do the flat spaces in between the teeth where they meet on the two rollers. Above the teeth on the smaller rollers, a third of the roller is exposed, and it is tapered little by little in two smaller circles covered with two iron hoops one and a half fingers thick and three fingers wide. The timber ends in a square sleeve of two or three *palmas* made of *sapupita-mirim* wood. This sleeve also holds the ends of the iron axle and is about three *palmas* around and the thickness of a roofing beam. It is installed with the force of an iron hammer. In order for the bushing and the sleeve to be more securely fixed in place, the four corners of the sleeve are held in place with tongue-and-groove joints re-enforced by small pieces of iron hammered in place. In order to hold it in place and keep it from shaking, small wedges of *lei* wood are inserted. In the same way, by tapering the ends with iron bands, sleeves, and axles that we have described for the two top ends of the smaller rollers, this is done for the lower parts of all three rollers. All three axles or centers of the rollers are encased with iron bushings the thickness of apples. The upper part of the axle is inserted in the bushing to a depth of two fingers, whereas the lower part is laid by its tip on two other pieces of flat iron that one calls the bushing or pivot, which is one *palma* long. It is also sheathed in iron so that it cannot be pierced by the ceaseless turns made by the end of the axle. All these three axles or rollers, where the ends meet the bushings, rest on a board called the "bridge," which is fifteen or sixteen *palmas* long. In order to hold the rollers securely, there are four supports about nine *palmas* high and seven thick, similar in their function to those that support the high beams and *porca,* or beam with a hole in it, holding the axle of the main roller. It rises to an elevation above the other rollers and forms the main part of the mill. Resting on these supports from one end to the other are boards called *mesas* that are almost one *palma* thick and twenty long. On these are the cross-beams called *gatos,* where the upper part of the rollers turn. On top of these there is another equally long layer of boards called "needles" that secure the wedges that hold the rollers in place.

The bundles of cane that are about to be pressed between the rollers are placed on two boards, one on each side of the rollers. They are secured by semicircles around the edge of the rollers, secured to them without getting in the way of their rotations. These boards are next to the rollers in order to prevent the cane or the pressed stocks from falling near the axles and slowing in some way the rollers, and to keep the juice from the cane clean and not pollute the *caldo*.[14]

CHAPTER VI

How the Cane Is Milled and the Number of People Required to Mill It

THE CANE IS PRESSED by pushing stalks, free of leaves and mud (and if necessary, it can be washed) between two rollers where the turning of the rollers will crush it. The rollers move by the power of interlocking teeth. Once the cane has passed through the rollers, the stalks are then passed once again to extract as much liquid as possible from them. This liquid (the *caldo*) falls from the rollers to a wooden vat that is placed underneath the rollers, and from that point it flows to a tub placed in the ground, called the *caldo* vat. From there it is lifted up in two kettles or pipes with a hoist, wheel, rollers, and chains, and the *caldo* is poured into another kettle on an elevated platform. This is called the hoisting kettle. From there it moves to the kettle house, where it will be refined.

In a period of twenty-four hours, the mill presses one *tarefa redonda* of twenty-five to thirty cartloads of cane. In one week, in those called "single" (which means not counting the Holy Day), the mill can press seven *tarefa redondas*. The expected production is one loaf[15] of sugar for each day's task. That is, a task is the amount of cane one pair of slaves can cut and bundle in one day. Making more sugar does not depend on milling more cane; what counts is if the cane has a lot of sweet liquid and is not soggy or old. If they process more cane or pressed stalks than they can handle, there is a risk of damaging the smaller water wheel and the control of the rollers, damaging the flywheel, or possibly breaking an axle. If a lot of water is passing over the wheel, it will mill so much cane that the cauldrons will not be able to contain it and the liquid [*caldo*] will sour in the first vat because they cannot cook so much liquid fast enough. For this reason, the overseer at the mill and the sugar master have to keep the process running smoothly to avoid wasting the cut cane.

The most dangerous place in the entire mill is at the rollers. If by bad luck, the female slave feeding the cane into the rollers, due to lack of sleep or any other lack of attention, inadvertently sticks her hand farther into the rollers than she should, she risks being crushed between the rollers. This is unless her hand or arm is immediately cut off. For this purpose, there is a large knife at the mill. They will have to use the knife unless they have not been slow to use the brake to stop the wheel. The use of the brake diverts the water from filling the cavities in the wheel and turning it. Help in one form or another quickly arrives to the afflicted. This danger is even greater at night than during the day; milling is done at both times. The planter alternates the teams who work feeding the rollers. These teams are mostly the unskilled slaves or those who usually get drunk.

At least seven or eight female slaves are required at the milling house. Three more are needed to bring in the cane, one to feed the rollers, another to feed the pressed cane for the second time, and another to position and light the oil lamps. There are five of these, and this last slave also cleans out the channel for the *caldo* (this slave is called the channel cleaner, or the *calumbá*) and the axles of the rollers and cools them with water so they do not overheat. To do this she uses the water container under the smaller wheel that collects the water falling from the axle, and slaves also use it to wash the mud from the cane. One more slave is needed to toss out the pressed stalks of cane, either to throw them into the river or on the trash pile to burn when it is convenient. If it is necessary to take the stalks farther away, one female slave is not sufficient. Someone will need to assist her. Otherwise, there will not be sufficient time to empty the mill house of the pressed stalks, and they will get in the way.

Regarding the vat for the *caldo*, which as we have said, is in the ground, there is a hoister who constantly lifts the *caldo* in two pipes. All of these female slaves need others to replace them once they have completed their shifts, which end at noon and midnight. All of them together wash all the rollers every twenty-four hours with brushes made of *piaçaba*.[16] The task for the hoisting slaves is to lift and empty each of three kettles, when they are full, into the cauldrons. Then another empties another three. In this way, they follow each other and can endure the work. The supervisor watches over all this more carefully than the others to ensure the smooth functioning of the mill. In addition to him, there is a guard or someone vigilant at the mill, whose job is to be alert and act for the supervisor. He works off and on during the day and night and ensures the cane is pressed correctly and crushed between the rollers. He also ensures that the crushed stalks are discarded, and that the axles as well as the braces are kept cool and cleaned. In the event of some accident occurring at the mill, he is the one who quickly brings it to a halt.

CHAPTER VII

The Wood Used to Make the Rollers, and
All Other Woodworking on the Plantation,
Canoes and Boats, and What Is Normally Paid
to Carpenters and Similar Workers

BEFORE TURNING FROM the mill to the furnaces and the cooking house, I think it necessary to discuss the timbers and wood that make up the mill and all the other woodworking on the plantation. In Brazil, it is possible to select the best types of wood, since there is no other place on Earth with an equally rich variety of select and strong wood. Only the best *lei* wood is used in the mill because experience has shown it to be the most suitable. *Lei* woods are the strongest, longest lasting, and best suited, and these include the *sapucaia, sapupira, sapupira-cari, sapupira-mirim, sapupira-açu, vinhático, arco,* yellow *jetaí,* the black *jetaí,* the *messetaúba, maçaranduba,* Brazil wood, *jacarandá, pau de oleo, picaí,* and other similar woods.[17] The wood used in the milling house, the furnace area, the cooking house, and the refining area should be *maçaranduba,* because it is very hard and works for everything. It is suitable for tie beams, roof beams, smaller roof beams, cross-beams or framework for the roof, dowels, and timber. This type of wood is found all around the *Recôncavo* and the coastline of Brazil. The large tie beams and roof beams are worth three to four *milréis,* sometime more depending on their length and width. These prices are for the timbers in their rough state as they arrive from the forest with only their first hewing. The rollers of the mill are made of *sapucaia* or of *sapupira-cari;* the top of the large roller is made from *pau d'arco* or *sapupira;* the pegs for the three rollers, the small wheel, and the flywheel are made of *messetaúba.* The water wheel is made of *pau d'arco, sapupira,* or *vinhático.* The curved sections of the small wheel, the flywheel, the beams, and cross-beams are made from *sapupira.* The supports and stands can be made of any of the *lei* woods. The carts are made of *sapupira-mirim, jetaí*, or *sapucaia*. The water trough is made from *vinhático*. The canoes are made from *picaí, joairana, jequitibá, utussica,* or *angelim*. The ribbing and cross-sections of the boats are made from *sapupira, landim-carvalho,* or *sapupira-mirim*. The keel is made from *sapupira* or from *peroba,* the sheathing and broadsides from *utim, peroba, buranhém,* and *unhuíba*. The masts are made from *inhuibatam,* the spars from *camaçari,* the rudder from *averno* or *angelima,* the curves and arcs of the bow and poop from *sapupira,* as are the cross-beams on the deck. The barge poles are made from white mangrove, and the oars from *lindirana* or of *jenipapo*.

The crates in which the sugar is packed are made from *jequitibá* and *camaçari*. If there is not enough of these two types of wood, *burissica* can be used for the tops and bottoms. The boards for the crates come from the sawmill already cut, and at the mill they only gather them, put them in order, and smooth the edges, as it is not necessary to have the sides in place. These are two and a half *palmas* high and seven and a half or eight *palmas* wide, and the bottom pieces are three *palmas* by the same length. In past years, crates were worth ten or twelve *tostões,* but their price is higher nowadays.

The axle of the roller, in its rough natural state, cut only on the ends or hewn to eight sides, is worth forty or fifty, or even sixty *milréis* or more, depending upon the quality of the wood and how much it is needed. Those from Porto Seguro and Patipe are inferior because they come from the lowlands. The best are those from Pitanga and the new lands above Santo Amaro. The costs for wood for the mill are more than one thousand *cruzados,* not counting the water wheel. Since it is constructed with bolts and cavities, it is worth more than two hundred *milréis*.

The carpenter on the mill receives five *tostões* daily if he is not also fed. If he is also given meals, then he receives a *cruzado* and even more these days, since all the prices have gone up. The carpenters doing the lighter work on the plantation receive almost as much. The carpenters working on the boats and the caulkers receive seven and a half *tostões* without meals, six *tostões* or two *patacas* if meals are included.[18] A boat rigged to carry firewood or crates of sugar costs five hundred *milréis*. A boat to transport sugarcane is three hundred *milréis,* and a *rodeira* costs four hundred *milréis*. The price of the canoes depends on their size and the type of wood from which they are made. For these reasons, those used on the mills are both large and small, and the price for these is both high and low—that is, twenty, thirty, forty, or fifty *milréis*.

The timber is cut in the wild with axes all year long except during special phases of the moon, three days before the new moon or three days after it is full. Timber is removed from the wild in different ways. In the lowlands, some of the timbers are rolled on other logs and slaves haul other logs. On the hills, they lower them with ropes. On higher elevations, they drag them. This is done when oxen cannot be used because the land is too steep or the woods are in a depression, full of holes. However, when the oxen can pull the logs, they remove them harnessed with ropes or thick vines or leather straps, tied to the harnesses and carefully secured with pins. During the rainy season, they say hauling is easier in the mud than during the dry season, because the rains make it easier for the logs to slide along.

CHAPTER VIII

Furnaces, Their Equipment, the Required Firewood, and the Ash Used for Leaching

Next to the milling house, which is also called the building for the mill, is the building for the furnaces. These are actually consuming mouths that inhale wood from the countryside, black holes of perpetual fire and smoke giving lively images of the volcanoes of Mounts Vesuvius and Etna. One might almost say the furnace looks like Purgatory or Hell. Near the furnaces there are those condemned to work them, which are the slaves with yaws[19] and those with an imbalance in their humors that ties them to this tiring work in order to purge themselves by their prodigious sweat of the acidic humors filling their bodies. Other slaves can be seen there, the wicked and perverse, locked in long and heavy iron chains in this demanding work. They pay for their wicked excesses with little or no hope of mending their ways.

On the royal mills, there are usually six furnaces and numerous additional assisting slaves called firewood stokers. The openings for the furnaces are ringed with iron. This is not only to give more support for the bricks but also to prevent the stokers from causing an accident when they feed the fire. At its mouth, each furnace has two holes that are vents allowing the fire to puff and blow. The pillars between them have to be very strong, made of brick and baked lime, but the body of the furnace is made from bricks with clay to better resist the intense heat of the fire. Neither baked lime nor hard stone will do this. The cauldrons are a bit larger than the kettles. The source for the fire is wood. Only Brazil, with its vast stretches of countryside, can supply the needs of so many furnaces. It has done this for many years and will do so for many more in the future. How many furnaces there are on the mills of Bahia, Pernambuco, and Rio de Janeiro that operate day and night, six, seven, eight, and nine months of the year! To understand how abundant this countryside is, just the region around Jaguaripe provides sufficient firewood for the many mills along the coast of the *Recôncavo* of Bahia.[20] In reality, it supplies almost all those in that region. They begin to cut firewood in Jaguaripe in July because the mills in Bahia start milling in August.

Each slave must cut and pile daily a measure of wood seven *palmas* high and eight long. This is also the size of a cart, and eight carts makes one *tarefa*. Cutting the wood, arranging, transporting, and loading it onto the boat are tasks for the wood seller. Arranging it on board is the responsibility of the sailors. There are boats able to haul five *tarefas*; some carry four, some three, and each *tarefa* costs 2,500 *réis* when the master of the mill sends his boat to seek it. If the seller brings the wood in his boat, then the cargo charges are added according to the distance from the port. A royal mill in production eight or nine months from one year to another spends 2,000 *cruzados* for firewood. There was one year when the Sergipe do Conde Mill spent more than 3,000 *cruzados* because it milled longer than usual and the price of the firewood was higher. The firewood is transported in sailboats, with four sailors and the boat master. For the smooth operation of the mill, the master should have two boats, since when one arrives, the other can depart to collect more firewood. The best mix of firewood is half big, thick logs and cross-pieces, which are smaller, and the other half small pieces. The big pieces feed the furnaces and cook the sugar in the cauldrons, where it is necessary to have a hotter fire for the sugar to coagulate. The medium-size pieces feed the fires made from the bigger pieces, while the smaller pieces are used under the kettles where they skim the *caldo*. In order to clean out the dregs from the *caldo*, it is necessary to have continuous flames. For that reason, the big pieces are called "cauldron firewood" and the smaller pieces are called "kettle firewood."

After the firewood has arrived at the dock for the mill, it is stacked in a pile. It is always a good idea to have five or six *tarefas* of firewood piled in front of or near the furnaces. Two boatloads of cane normally require one of wood, assuming the wood has been sorted, since if it is only smaller pieces it will not be enough. The first preparation of the firewood to start the fire for the furnaces is called "setting." This involves shifting the larger logs and putting them in the bottom of the furnace (this is done with large poles called *transfogueiros*),[21] and then placing smaller cross-pieces of firewood on top of these. In this way, the fire grows higher and the flames closer to the bottom of the cauldrons and kettles. The person feeding the fire has to obey those tending the cauldrons. He must feed the fire exactly as those above him communicate the need for wood. This is to prevent the *caldo* or *melado* (see chart) from boiling over the copper kettles, as well as to provide sufficient heat to make it boil. If it does not boil at the right time, it will not be possible to skim off the impurities that need to rise to the top. The impurities can be removed and the liquid can be cleaned in the cauldrons. Therefore, in regard to the boiling pans, the greater the fire the better.

The ash from the furnaces is used for leaching. It purifies the *caldo* in the kettles and helps make the sugar stronger. In order to do this, a slave takes an iron rod and pulls ash and cinders to the mouth of the furnace. From there, the slave uses an iron shovel to remove them and take them to the ash box, which is a tank made of brick on pillars made of stone and lime, in a square with walls around it. It is here that the ash is kept hot, and while hot it is added to the vats. In order to do this, the vats are placed on a support three *palmas* high. Then the mixture is stirred and blended. Then boiling water is added from one of the large kettles on a fire near the ash tank. This water comes from the pipe to the kettle house. This water is stirred with the ashes until its passes through the holes in the bottom of the kettle. It then fills the half-buried forms or vessels. From these, the water is removed with a coconut shell and put in a kettle in the kettle house. From there, it goes into the forms placed between the cauldrons, and it is used by the cauldron workers in the *caldo,* as will be described later.

It is important to note that not all types of firewood are suitable for leaching. Neither the hardwood nor wood that is dry will work. The reasons for this are that hardwood makes more charcoal than ash, and the small pieces provide little ash and the ash is weak. The best wood for ash is white mangrove and softer woods — that is, wood from the cashew, pepper, and fig trees. In order to know if the ash for leaching is perfect, it is necessary to place a drop on the finger and taste it. If it burns, it will be good; if it does not, it will be weak. They also make extra ash and keep it from one year to the next in the tanks where it is usually stored. Before putting it into the vats, it should be reheated in the ash box or mixed with the first ashes from the furnaces with some cinders. If it has lost its strength, this will invigorate it.

CHAPTER IX

The Cauldrons and Copper Vessels, Their
Organization, the Skilled Workers and Others
Required, and the Tools They Use

T HE THIRD PART of this building above the furnaces is the area
for the copper vessels. Even though this structure is commonly
called the House of the Cauldrons, there are not only the copper con-
tainers there. There are also large vessels such as the kettles, pots, and
boiling pans. On royal mills, they have two production lines of these
vessels in operation to handle the quantity of *caldo* coming from the
rollers. These copper vessels sit atop the dome of the furnace on supports or collars with brick and lime around them. These are open in
such a way that the bottom of the vessel is inside the furnace. Each
of these sits atop the opening holding it. Each extends down into its
opening according to its size. The boiling pans are not as deep, and the
cauldrons are a lot deeper. There is a wall separating one section from
another, and another wall separating the building for the furnaces from
another next to the mill. In front, they have one or two steps that the
slaves climb in order to work from these with the necessary instruments
in their hands. This arrangement provides sufficient space to control
the vessels from a greater height and distance. All around the wall in
front of them, with a path cleared in the middle, is the cooling shed
where the cooked sugar is poured into molds to congeal. It can hold
eighty molds or more.

One complete series of copper vessels (in addition to the *caldo* kettle
and the hoisting kettle, which are in the mill house) consists of two
cauldrons, one called the *meio* and the other the *melar,* a kettle for
skimming, a great kettle called the *melado* kettle, and a smaller one
called the filtering kettle. This is followed by a series of four boiling
pans: one to receive, one at the door, one for cooking, and one to whisk
the liquid. At the end, a smaller pot is used to pour the condensed

liquid sugar into the molds. Other larger and smaller copper vessels are used in a similar process.

The *caldo* kettle on a royal mill is made from twenty *arrobas* of copper. The hoisting kettle is made from another twenty. The two cauldrons are made from sixty *arrobas,* the skimming kettle is made of twelve *arrobas* of copper, the *melado* kettle from fifteen *arrobas,* and the filtering kettle is from eight *arrobas.* The series of four boiling pans is made from nine *arrobas* each, or thirty-six *arrobas.* The small pot is made from four. Altogether, this is 175 *arrobas* of copper. Once it is worked and prepared, when it is cheap, it sells for 400 *réis* per pound. This is 2,240$00 *milréis,* or 5,600 *cruzados.* If another production line is added with smaller or equal copper vessels, its cost will be in relation to their sizes.[22]

The part of the cauldrons and boiling pans that suffers the most through this constant use is the bottom. If the vessel is made of poor quality copper or it is not thick enough, it will not be possible to refine the *caldo* as required in the cauldrons and the fire will burn the sugar in the boiling pans before it can be cooked and whisked. Because of this, the royal mills, which work seven or eight months a year, repair and remake all the bottoms of the cauldrons and boiling pans.

The person who presides over the entire effort in this section is the sugar master. It falls to his judgment if the *caldo* has been refined, if the sugar cooked and whisked in the quantities he requests, based on his judgment. He helps in adjusting the three needed temperatures for processing the *melado* and pouring the liquid into the molds. This is in addition to what he has to do in the refinery, which we will discuss in its correct sequence. His main assistant helps during the day; when night falls, the *banqueiro* takes on this job. He is the foreman of this section. Making good or bad sugar depends largely on the intelligence, experience, and vigilance of these two. Even if the cane is not what it should be, skill can provide what nature did not. On the other hand, it is of little importance that the cane might be good if the liquid taken from it and all the hard work are wasted because of carelessness. This would place not a small burden on the conscience of someone receiving a generous salary. The *banqueiro* also has to pour the sugar into the molds at night, put them into the shed, and arrange rushes [grasses] around them. To assist him in performing these last two chores, during the day there is the assistant *banqueiro*. He divides the sugar into the molds, organizes them in the shed, and arranges them as described.

Eight people alternately work the cauldrons, divided into two teams. One is at each cauldron working continuously until handing it over to the next person, skimming the boiling *caldo* [condensed liquid sugar] with vessels and ladles. Each person working the cauldrons has to skim three cauldrons for *caldo,* which occurs in three successive phases called *meladuras.* The last of these is called "the handing over," since it must be half-refined when turned over to the next person. For these three *meladuras,* the female hoisting slave (the *guindadeira*)[23] gives each the *caldo* as it is required; after one *meladura* has been skimmed and refined, she gives them one *caldo* to process into another batch of *meladura.*[24]

At the kettles, four people work in teams; one is in each line of the kettles. Each of them must cook and whisk as much sugar as is needed to fill a *venda*[25] of molds, which is four or five of them.

Finally, one female slave sweeps the area, positions and lights the six lamps (which use fish oil), removes the second- and third-stage dregs from their kettles, and returns them to the cauldrons. She has the nickname of *calcanha.*

This is also a house of penitents, because normally one sees mulattoes and locally born *negros* working at the boiling pans or cauldrons with big chains tied to a block. Some are runaways, or by the signs one can see what other malice they have done. The iron chains and the work pacify them. However, among them there are sometimes those who are not as guilty and are even innocent, because the master too easily believed what was told to him, or he is very vengeful or cruel.

The implements used in the furnace house are skimmers, ladles, great ladles, vessels, strainers, dividers, kettles, long brushes, whisking rods, taps, iron digging tools, spatulas, and lances. The large skimmers and ladles are used at the cauldrons. The skimmers are for cleaning out the impurities, and the ladles are for moving the *caldo* from one cauldron to another or to a kettle. For this reason, the handles of both are fourteen or fifteen *palmas* long, so the slaves can manipulate them. The great ladles are for putting water and leaching water into the cauldrons and to help the kettle workers pour the sugar into the divider

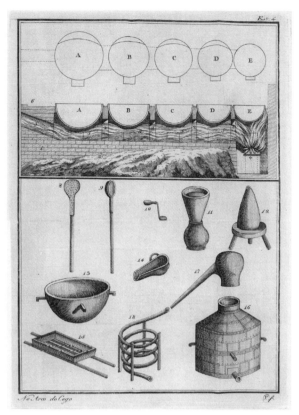

José Mariano da Conceiçao Velloso,
"Sugar-making Equipment," Lisbon, 1798
(JCB 72–196–9). Courtesy of the John Carter
Brown Library at Brown University

and afterward into the molds. The smaller skimmers, the whisking rods, strainers, and brooms are required by those working the large boiling pans. The divider, iron digging tool, and spatulas are used by the *banqueiro* and his assistant. The *calcanha* uses the large boiling pans, vessels, and taps to skim her own kettle and to put it into the cauldron. The broom is used to clean the impurities from around the edge of the kettles. The lance is for removing the sugar stuck in the kettles, and the iron digging tool makes the depressions in the stocks of pressed cane used to hold the molds in the cooling shed.

CHAPTER X

Cleaning and Purifying the Caldo *from the
Cane in the Cauldrons and the Filtering Kettle
until It Reaches the Boiling Pans*

THE JUICE FROM THE sugarcane makes its way from the hoist-ing kettle in a stream into the furnace house. The first place it goes is to a cauldron, the *meio* cauldron. In it, the *caldo* begins to boil and throw off the impurities that come with it from the mill. The fire at this point is doing its work, and the *caldo* yields its first skimming, called *cachaça*.[26] Because this is so full of little pieces, it goes away from the furnace house, over the edges of the cauldrons, which have lots of bricks around them, into a pipe buried in the ground. It is fed through a wooden trough within the brick edging around the cauldron. The *caldo* moves through this pipe to a large wooden trough to feed the animals. Goats, sheep, and pigs eat it, and in some places, even the oxen lick it. Everything that is sweet is delicious, even when it is filled with bits and pieces. In order that the fire does not stir up the froth more than necessary, and to allow the *caldo* to be skimmed, which is good, from time to time the cauldron workers add some water using a great ladle. In this way, the great force of heat from boiling is reduced and the impure *caldo* becomes clean.

The first skimming having left on its own, those at the cauldrons begin to skim the *caldo* using giant iron skimmers and "help" it. Adding from time to time a great ladle of water and ash is called "helping" the *caldo*. These are kept nearby; the water is in the tubs, and the leaching water is in the molds. The water cleanses the *caldo*, and the leaching water ensures the impurities at the bottom of the cauldron rise more quickly to the top and do not settle on the bottom. The leaching water also helps the sugar to condense and makes it stronger, mixing with the *caldo* in the way that salt blends with water. This second skimming is retained and channeled by another pipe from the same trough in the brick edging around the cauldron to a kettle below, removed from the fire. This is called the skimming kettle. From here, it is returned to the same cauldron to be refined by a *negra* woman (known as the *calcalha*)[27] using a vessel and kettle. They call this "passing again." It moves through a wooden pipe positioned on a brace at the same height as the cauldrons. They call this a "violin," since it has the shape of one. And then the *caldo* falls into the cauldron. When the *caldo* appears purified (which can be determined by the foam, by the large and small bubbles that arise, each time smaller and brighter) with the use of a great ladle (which is a copper concave receptacle with a wooden handle twelve or fifteen *palmas* long), the liquid is poured into the second cauldron. This is the *melar* cauldron, and it is here that the purification process is completed, with the same applications of water and leaching water, until the *caldo* is completely pure. The *caldo* is normally refined in the *meio* cauldron for about half an hour. After it is half-refined, it goes to the *melar* cauldron where it remains for an hour or hour and a quarter, until the skimming is complete. The cauldrons are never completely emptied of the *caldo* because that would damage them. Two or three *palmas* of liquid are left in the cauldron, and the new *caldo* is poured on top. The skimmings from this second cauldron are ladled into the skimming kettle and from there to the first or second cauldron until the end of the *tarefa*. From these skimmings, the *negros* make their *garapa*,[28] which is the drink they enjoy most and which they exchange with their equals for cassava flour, bananas, and beans. The *garapa* is stored in jugs until it loses its sweetness and turns sour, because that is when they say it is best for drinking. God willing, they will drink it in moderation and not until they get drunk. The next to last skimming from the last *meladura*, which is the last refining from the *caldo*, is called *claros*. Mixed with cold water, it is a delightful, refreshing drink that quenches the thirst during quiet times. Finally, when the sugar master decides the *meladura* has been completely refined, those working the cauldrons use a ladle to move the *caldo*, which at this point is called *mel*, from the great kettle, called the *melado* kettle. This kettle is not on the fire but next to the cauldron. The *mel* goes into the filtering kettle, which is smaller, with

The various stages of sugar production, according to Antonil.

Name and Type of Vessel	Weight in *Arrobas* of Copper	Name of Product	Skimmings	Processing Time
caldo cauldron	20	sugarcane juice		
hoisting cauldron	20	sugarcane juice		three cauldrons in 12 hours
meio cauldron	30	*caldo*	first: *cachaça*— fed to animals; second: retained	30 minutes
melar cauldron	30	*caldo*		about 1 hour to 1 hour 15 minutes
skimming kettle	12			not stated
melado kettle	15		*mel*	not stated
filtering kettle	8		*melado*	not stated
boiling pan to receive melado	9	*melado*	*netas* (second quality sugar)	short time
boiling pan at door	9			longer
boiling pan for cooking	9			
boiling pan for whisking	9	*mel/ melado*		three temperings: to begin, to equalize, and to fill
pouring pot molds	4			

filtering cloth extended over a grate. To prevent any liquid from spilling as it passes from one kettle to another and being lost, there is a curved tile attached to the edges of both of the kettles. It catches any liquid, which then is returned to one kettle or the other. This way, not a drop is lost of the sweet liquid created by so much sweat, blood, and tears.

CHAPTER XI

How Melado *Is Cooked and*
Whisked *in the Boiling Pans*

NOW THAT THE *caldo* has been refined and filtered, it goes to the boiling pans to be cooked, helped by a greater fire and flame than that needed in the cauldrons. The bottoms of the boiling pans have a greater thickness to allow the additional activity required at this stage. If the *melado* boils to the point where it threatens to spill over, throw in some animal fat and it will subside and become quiet. This also might be good advice for a person, should his indignation get out of control. They say that if any acidic liquid is added to the cauldrons or the boiling pans, for example lemon juice or something similar, the *melado* will never coagulate, nor will it solidify as it should. There is talk that this has happened. However, this does not appear to be correct, at least in reference to any acidic liquid other than lemon juice. There have been those who added a lot of sour *cachaça* to the *caldo*. Perhaps they did this as a practical joke, or because they were annoyed, or irritated. In spite of this, the sugar coagulated quite well when it was supposed to. Just because of the actions of some souls, their petty dissatisfactions cause all these efforts to amount to nothing. What is certain is that when the *melado* or the *mel* moves to the boiling pans, extreme vigilance and awareness are required from those working the boiling pans, the *banqueiro,* the assistant *banqueiro,* and the sugar master. This is when the sugar master uses his training and where extreme caution and skill are needed.

The *melado* leaves the filtering kettle for the awaiting boiling pans and goes to each one, staying in each as long as is required, and no longer, to complete a stage in the process. In the first boiling pan, called the "receiving," it boils and begins to cook, and the smallest impurities are removed. These are called *netas* and they are removed with a small skimmer into a mold placed there. If they want to use them, which is good, at the end of the week they make a second quality loaf of sugar.

These skimmings are not returned to the boiling pan in the way that they are earlier when *caldo* is returned to the cauldrons. From the receiving pan, where the liquid remains only a short time, the *melado* is moved with a copper ladle (made from a small skimmer) to a second boiling pan called "of the door." Here it continues to boil and thicken and any impurities are removed at the edge with a special broom, which is like a brush or a broom made of bark, with a twig holding the ends together. The *melado* stays in this boiling pan longer than in the first until it is half done. From here, it is moved with the same copper ladle, into the third boiling pan, called the "cooking pan." Even though it was cooking in the other pans, here the cooking is completed and it begins to condense perfectly until it is ready for whisking. The sugar master makes this judgment, or the *banqueiro* does so in his absence, judging by the shape and thickness of the *melado*. Having reached this stage, it is called *mel* at its peak, thick and sufficiently condensed and ready to move to the fourth boiling pan, called the "whisking pan," where it is whipped with a beater, similar to a skimmer with the same edges but no holes. It is whisked to keep it from burning. Once it has been whisked and cooked enough, the liquid is lifted with the same beaters as high above the boiling pan as they can. This is called "letting it breathe." In this process, those working the boiling pans demonstrate their special talents. They continue doing this, more or less, as demanded by the three temperings required of the sugar going into the molds. These temperings are so essential and demanding that it would be best to speak about them in the next chapter.

CHAPTER XII

The Three Temperings of Melado *and Its Correct Distribution in the Molds*

B EFORE THE *melado* goes into the molds, while still in the whisk-ing pan, it is necessary to adjust the cooking to the tempering demanded by the rule of good distribution. There are three, and each is different and each requires a different concoction. In the same way, by different means and with repeated reasons, we attempt to temper souls in the grip of any strong passion.

The first tempering is called "to begin" or "basin tempering." This consists of straight *mel*, because it has been cooked less. It is the first taken from the whisking pan right away, and it is put in a basin with the beater. The basin is not on the fire and is next to the boiling pans. It is mixed using a spatula or a great ladle with the mouth pointed down. The *banqueiro* or the assistant *banqueiro* has prepared four or five molds in the shed in a row of pressed stalks of cane. Each has its bottom hole filled and the mold is elevated. Four or five molds are what they call a *venda*. This tempering is poured using a great ladle inside a divider. The *mel* is divided among the four or five molds by the *banqueiro* or the assistant *banqueiro* or someone working the boiling pans. However, this is at the order of the sugar master, filling each with its portion that, with luck, will leave space for the other two temperings, which should follow immediately.

The second tempering is called "to equalize," and it involves more cooking since the *mel* was in the whisking pan longer. Stirred and thickened, it was also whisked more. This is also removed from the pans, placed into the basin, and stirred with a great ladle. It then goes into the four molds using the divider with an equal amount in each. This is stirred with spatulas more than the first tempering.

This is followed by the third and last tempering, called "to fill." The *mel* has all the cooking and thickness needed and is put in the basin and mixed with the great ladle, put in the divider, taken to the shed, and used to fill the molds. The three temperings are mixed together in the molds using a spatula and, with luck, the three will blend into one. This procedure is so critical that, without it, the sugar in the molds cannot later whiten and be refined. If they poured only perfectly cooked tempering into the molds, it would coagulate and condense in such a way that water could not filter through it and cleanse it after the top is sealed with clay. If the tempering was completely free of heating, it would fail to crystallize in the molds and collapse into *mel*. With the mixture of the three temperings, it coagulates in such as way that it stays firm while the water filters through it little by little, keeping the sugar dense and strong. The sugar is whitened without melting; the process is just enough to refine it perfectly. To find this middle way in accomplishing the temperings requires the best work and skill of the sugar master. In the same way, this is the major difficulty in the practice of virtue caught in the middle of two extreme vices.

Melado served on plates and in pots for eating is from the first and second temperings. *Melado* from the third tempering, well whisked in the divider, makes *rapaduras*,[29] so loved by children. It coagulates on a piece of paper with the four edges turned up as if they were walls, within which the *melado* hardens when cooled and is about the size of the palm of a hand. Happy is the boy who gets a couple of these. Licking those papers puts him in a much better mood than using them to practice his ABCs.

With this it will be understood why this sweet substance possesses so many different names before it attains the more noble and perfect name of "sugar." These names have to do with its beginnings, its processing, and its perfection, and describe various states through which it passes. Each state has a name that changes. So, at the mill it is called "sugarcane juice." Until it reaches the *meio* cauldron, it is called *caldo*. At that point, it is boiling *caldo*. At the *melar* cauldron, it is clarified. At the basin it is filtered. At the boiling pans, it is *melado*. Finally, after the tempering and in the molds it is "sugar." The different qualities of sugar we will discuss when we see it being packed in the crates.

The last skimmings of *meladura*, the *claros*, as we have said become *garapa* for the *negros*. These *claros* are alternately distributed in the following order. At the end of a *tarefa*, they are given to those working the cauldrons and the furnaces. At the end of the next, they are given to the slave women working at the mill. After that, they are for the crab and shrimp fishermen for them to share, and then to the boatmen who bring the cane and the wood to the mill. The distribution is always repeated in the same order. In this way, all of those who feel the burden of the work receive a jug of the nectar and ambrosia they desire.

When the order is given for the mill to stop on Sundays and Holy Days, the *melado* stuck at the bottom is removed from the boiling pans with an iron lance. The vats cannot be allowed to cool with the *melado* still present. In addition, they add water so that the copper vats do not burn. It also washes them, and that is how they leave them until the new *mel* arrives to be cooked.

[BOOK THREE]

CHAPTER I

Regarding the Molds for Sugar and Their Movement
from the Cooling Shed to the Refinery

T HE MOLDS USED FOR the sugar are vessels of clay fired in the
furnace. They resemble bells and are three and a half *palmas*
high and proportionally wide. They have a larger circumference at the
mouth and smaller at the end, which has a hole in it to allow the cleans-
ing and refining of the sugar. These molds were sold for four *vinténs,*[1]
except when they are in short supply. Not obtaining them in due time
causes their price to rise. Being made of poor quality clay or being
poorly fired in the kiln are major flaws, as is being too small. The good
quality molds are capable of turning out loaves weighing three and a
half *arrobas.* These molds have their cooling shed in the kettle house
filled with the crushed stalks of cane. These have a small trench made
within them by an iron or wooden hoe, and act as a bed or support for
two equal rows of molds. As we have already said, four or five molds
make a *venda.* Before putting any sugar into them, the hole at the bottom is plugged with a wad of banana leaves. The molds are secured in
place with rushes and wild canes to keep them from breaking once all
the sugar is poured inside. Then, the sugar is added in the three temperings as we have noted.

In the period of three days, the sugar in some molds hardens more
than in others. Where it hardens the most, it is very difficult to break.
This is called "sugar with a sealed top." The type of sugar that breaks
with any hit is called "sugar with an open top." These metaphors also
express the distinct and different natures and condition of men, some

so fragile and others who can endure. The sugar will be good or poor depending on the *vendas* consisting of more or fewer molds. For the sugar to turn out well and harden quickly, four molds are sufficient. For it to harden more slowly, six, seven, or eight molds are used. These are then filled, taking more time than the minimum to fill them, and this creates better granulation. These are then carried on the backs of slaves or in wheelbarrows to the refinery, which we will discuss shortly.

A royal mill with two production lines of kettles with a good amount of liquid from the cane will make more or less 200 loaves of sugar each six days. If the liquid is less, they will make 120 loaves. If the mill obtains less liquid, it is because the cane is old or watery. This demonstrates the clear proof that extremes of any kind are sinful.

CHAPTER II

Refining the Sugar in Its Molds

T HE REFINERY IS normally separated from the building housing the mill. The best of the many in the *Recôncavo* of Bahia without a doubt is on the Sergipe do Conde Mill. It is made with stone, lime, and timbers from the *maçaranduba* tree. This tidy scene is roofed with tile and measures some 446 *palmas* long and 86 wide. It is divided into three rows with platforms with twenty-six brick pillars in the middle, each fifteen and a half *palmas* high and four wide. These support the roof, which also rests on large, thick walls all around. This building has fifty-two windows to allow the necessary light and air to enter. These are eight *palmas* high and six wide, and there are twenty-three windows on each side, with three more at the front with a door and three at the rear. The platforms are composed of racks of planks with round openings astride brick pillars, seven *palmas* high. Each plank has ten of these openings to hold an equal number of molds. In this manner, when filled the refinery can accommodate up to two thousand loaves of sugar at the same time. Underneath these planks with their openings are other boards of the same width. These have little channels carved in them, and the front of these boards is raised. These channels act like conduits for the *mel* that drains from the holes in the molds, refining the sugar. It flows to buried tanks. In the end, there is a furnace with which to cook and transform this into sugar, with its cooling shed capable of holding forty molds. Also at the entrance, to the left of the door, is a little room made of wood to hold the sugar left over from crating. This room also contains the tools needed to plaster the clay, separate sugar, dry it, and crate it. At the front of the refinery, before the planks to hold the molds, is an area large enough to hold three hundred crates. It is a secure and sheltered area for crating with its door facing west. This allows it to absorb all the heat from the afternoon sun, sheltering the sugar from humidity—its worst enemy after it has been made and crated.

In front of the refinery, there is a veranda supported by six pillars. It is eighty-two *palmas* long and twenty-four wide. Underneath it is the counter for sifting sugar and a trough for mixing the clay that is plastered on the open tops of the molds to refine the sugar. Further on, there is the drying counter, some eighty *palmas* long and fifty-six wide. It is supported by twenty-five brick pillars that are higher in the middle with a sharp incline on the sides. This allows the water from the heavens to drain better and is a stronger construction. This building is also made from *lei* wood—that is, *maçaranduba* or *vinhático*—and the structure can cover sixty canvas cloths and at the same time dry many loaves of sugar.

The People Required to Refine, Separate, Dry, and Crate the Sugar; the Tools Needed to Do This

WHEN THERE IS NO refiner (and it is always a good idea to have one), the sugar master is in charge of the refinery. He judges when the first and second applications of clay are needed on the molds. It depends on the condition of the sugar when more or less moisture or sprinkling is required. He also decides when to remove the clay or the sugar from the molds. However, even when there is a special refiner, paid his salary, it is always a good idea for him to consult with the sugar master. This will allow him to work with greater assurance, and the two of them should communicate frequently so that the planter and the tenants are well served by their efforts. This will also promote their reputations as skilled in this profession.

The person in charge at the counter for separating, drying, weighing, and crating the sugar is the crater. It is his responsibility to divide and regulate with great accuracy and truth everything that occurs under his charge. He also nails the crates shut, marks them, and delivers them into the hands of their owners.

Four female slaves work in the refinery. They plaster and cover the sugar with clay while it is in the molds and give the sugar its washings. At the separating counter, there are two experienced female slaves, called "mothers of the counter." Together with others, they separate and sort the inferior sugar from the superior, bring the molds, and remove the loaves of sugar from them. There is also a *negro* man who kneads the clay used for refining.

At the drying counter, the same two "mothers" also work with their helpers, which might be up to ten women. They lay out the canvas cloths and hammer the chips and large clumps into smaller pieces. They work behind those initially breaking the loaves. In the crating area, male and female *negras* help the crater to weigh and crate the sugar. As many people as are needed work there as well in pounding and sorting the sugar and nailing and marking the crates.

Tools needed in the refinery are: boring rods made of iron to pierce the sugar in the center aligned with the plug; iron digging tools to dig a hole in the middle, before the first and second layers of clay are applied; and small wooden hammers used to cover the loaf with clay. At the separating counter, they use leather hides to hold the sugar loaves when they are dislodged from the molds. They also use knives and small axes in separating and hammers to break the *mascavado*[2] sugar. At the drying counter, they need knives, hammers, wooden rakes, and the breaking pole. It is flat on four sides and breaks the loaves of sugar. For weighing, they require a scale, weights of two *arrobas,* and other smaller ones, such as the weight used for calculating deductions, and shovels and large baskets. In the crating house, they use poles to pound, rakes, tamping poles and others, and a leveling spatula. In addition, they need an adze, drills, hammers, nails, crowbars to remove nails from the crates, and clamp irons to force together any split or open boards. The clamp iron digs its claws into the sides of the board while pulling with its teeth or arms, secured above, and pulls down the sides. They also need the branding irons to indicate the quality of the sugar, the number of *arrobas,* and the name of the mill from where it came. In this manner, any trade values its tools to make the work easier and ensure a job well done. Without these tools, the work cannot succeed or even have a chance.

CHAPTER IV

The Clay Used for the Sugar Molds; What Type
It Should Be, How It Should Be Kneaded, and If It
Is Wise to Have a Pottery Workshop on the Plantation

THE CLAY USED for refining the sugar comes from the *apicus*, which, as we have said, is the beach exposed at low tide and covered at high tide.[3] It is transported on boats, canoes, or rafts. These rafts are two canoes tied together with boards crossing them, with the clay piled on the boards. Once it arrives at the mill, the clay is put in a special place and from there it is dried in the furnace house on a wooden platform secured by two supports. This is called the *giro*[4] and is above the ash box when it is filled with ash and cinders. Even though it dries in fifteen days, it is left there as long as there is need for clay for the already filled molds, as will be explained in its proper place. Once dried, it is broken with hammers, which are wooden tools used for pounding. At that point it is thrown into an old canoe or large wooden trough. A *negro* man continues to mix it, using water, stirring it and kneading it with a wooden scraper. This is an unhappy task. The other slaves—those who cut and transport the cane, those working in the mill, those at the cauldrons and kettles, the refinery, and the drying shed—always have food nearby. Only this poor fellow and those who feed wood onto the fires work without food. Even though all receive a share of *garapa*, the tasks are demanding without this appeasement during the day. However, there is no lack of other slaves who pity their poor luck, giving them pieces of sugarcane, a little bit of *mel*, or some sugar. When compassion is lacking in the others, they (the slaves not receiving food) will not lack the resourcefulness to seek a remedy, taking what and where they can.

The indication that the clay has been kneaded correctly is that it will not have lumps, which are bits that have not dissolved. Once they are worked out, the clay is ready. When a piece of it is placed on a roofing tile or a piece of the mold, it stays on top and does not slip off. From the trough, the clay is removed with a gourd and put into the copper kettles. It is then taken to the refinery where a large copper ladle is used to remove it and place it on the molds when the proper time arrives, as will be explained later.

Some feel that having a pottery workshop on a plantation saves more money than it costs, since there is a constant demand on the plantation for molds, bricks, and roofing tiles. On the other hand, some feel differently because a pottery uses a lot of firewood in its kiln to heat and fire the clay, and firing must be done using mangrove wood. When this is removed, it causes the destruction of the habitat for shellfish, which are a godsend for the slaves. In addition to this, a pottery requires the labor of six or seven *peças* [slaves]. They can be put to better use in the cane fields or at the mill, rather than at the pottery workshop, with its wages, potter's wheel, and other equipment as well as the need to obtain the clay at the beach where it originates. All this is expensive. For much less, the planter can purchase the molds and tiles that he needs. The best advice is for the planter to place one male slave born in Brazil in some unaffiliated pottery workshop, since he will be given half of what he produces. In a year he will make up to three thousand molds. The planter can use these and spend little. As a result, the planter will have many slaves, plenty of firewood, and mangroves with more than sufficient shellfish. He will also have pottery, and this will further the magnitude, convenience, and smooth running of the mill.

CHAPTER V

How Sugar Is Refined in the Molds and
How It Is Treated in the Refinery

T HE MOLDS ARE brought into the refinery and put on boards with holes cut to hold them. The plug that was placed in the bottom of the molds in the cooling shed is removed. With a pointed iron rod two and a half *palmas* long, they are pierced with blows using a small wooden hammer. Once they are pierced, the molds are arranged and placed on the boards, which are called "those with holes" [drainboards]. They pierce each mold and make sure it is secure. They are left for fifteen days with no clay covering them. They begin to refine themselves, and the drops fall from the holes in the bottom. The first *mel* that flows from the molds into the channels goes into a tank. This *mel* is inferior and at wintertime it is given to the slaves. Each slave is given one kettleful, and two are given to each couple. This is the best minimal amount and is also the best comfort they have. However, others cook it or sell it to those who make white *batido*[5] sugar from it, or distill it into rum.

After the fifteen days have passed, the clay can safely be applied and it is done in the following way. Four female slave refiners carve with metal carvers in the middle of the face of the loaf (which is the top) of the dry sugar. They quickly smooth it out with small wooden hammers and cover it with the first layer of clay. The clay is removed from the copper pots with large ladles. The pots come full from the trough where the clay was kneaded to the correct consistency. The slaves use their palms to spread the clay over the face (top) of the mold until it is two fingers deep. The second or third day, they pour half a ladle or a cup and a half of water over the top of the mold. In order to avoid directly hitting the clay and making a hole in it, the slave catches the water poured from the right hand with her left hand. The slave holds her hands over the clay and spreads water equally over the surface. The slave then uses her right hand to very lightly spread the water over the clay in such a way that her fingers do not disturb the clay on the face of the sugar. This treatment is called "humidifying," "sprinkling," or "giving it washings," or also "giving it humidity." The first layer of clay gets only one of these and remains on the face of the mold for six days, when it is dry and is then removed. The face is then dug again in the middle just as was done the first time and it is covered again with the same care and a second layer of clay is applied. It will remain on the mold for fifteen days and will receive six, seven, or more treatments of humidifying, depending on the quality of the sugar. Stronger sugar needs more applications, since it resists the water refining it. Sometimes it requires nine or ten applications. If the sugar has not congealed as much and is weak, it takes the water directly and is refined right away. When this is the case the planter is not pleased, since he would rather have stronger sugar than one refined so quickly. Also, in the summer, it is necessary to have more washings. That is, they must be done every two or every three days, depending on how hot it is. It is important to apply these washings before the heat causes cracks to open in the clay. In the winter, the first layer of clay is left for six days. Some do not give it any washings other than what the clay alone provides, especially during rainy days. However, once the first layer is removed and the second is in place, it is given six, seven, or eight applications every three days depending on the quality of the sugar and on the results of these washings.

As the sugar is being refined, it is also getting whiter in degrees. That is, it is getting whiter at the top, less so in the middle, very little toward the bottom, and not at all at the feet, which are called *cabuchos*. This darker, less refined sugar is called *mascavado*. Also, since it is being refined, the sugar is getting lower and lower in the mold, and it is becoming refined very slowly. It lowers only as far as half a *palma*, which is called the "size of a key," and is the length from the base of the thumb to the end of the index finger. If this happens, the refining will be good and a good amount of strong sugar will result. However, if it is refined quickly, it will result in less sugar.

The speed with which the sugar is refined in the molds, quickly or slowly, results partly from the quality of the cane, whether it is bad or good. It is also important that the cooking and temperings be done correctly. If the sugar is overcooked, it will be too dense and will never refine correctly. It will not be affected by the applications of water. This is not because it is strong but because it is overcooked. This shows itself by the lack of refining and by the clay not percolating down the molds. On the other hand, if the sugar is undercooked and the temperings were too short, it will mostly decompose into *mel* as the liquid passes through it. Another problem is when the loaves of sugar have "eyes," which is when the white sugar has veins of *mascavado* in it. Some say this results from poor applications of water on the clay while in the molds. Others believe it results from the temperings being too hot or too cold, or from unequal distribution of the *mel* in the molds.

The *mel* that drips from the molds after moisture has been applied to the clay is channeled to kettles and tubs, where it is cooked and whisked. The sugar made from this process is called white *batido*. It also produces a *mascavado*, called *mascavado batido*, or it can be distilled into rum. I never recommend a planter do this (make rum), so that he will avoid continual unrest in the slave quarters. His male and female slaves will get even more drunk on rum than if they drink *cachaça*.

The first layer of clay put on top of the molds is two fingers thick. When it is dry and removed after six days, it is only one finger thick. When the second application is removed (which was also originally two fingers thick) after fifteen days, it is only half a finger thick. Now that the sugar has been refined, the washings have also stopped. Three or four days after the last of these, the second layer of clay, now dry, is removed. After it is gone, the molds are given eight more days to complete their drying and refining. At that point, they can be removed. The clay is not without admiration for being itself. By its nature it is impure, yet is an instrument of purity for the sugar by its washings. Just as the clay acts on the sugar, it is with tears that impure souls are purified and cleansed.

CHAPTER VI

How Sugar Is Removed from the
Molds, Separated, and Dried

WHEN THE TIME has come to remove the sugar from the molds, on a very clear day as many people as possible work at the drying counter. The molds are brought on the backs of slaves or in wheelbarrows from the refinery to the separating tables. It is very important that the selected day be very clear, since if the sugar absorbs any humidity, even if later dried in the sun, it will never return to the perfect state it had previously. In a similar way, leftover sugar from one year loses its cohesion and whiteness, and it can never regain them. This is the nature of purity: once it is offended it can never return to what it had been. The person in charge of these activities is the crater, and he is responsible for all I am about to relate. At the bottom of the separating table, the molds are arranged on leather hides. The hide is moved back and forth very slowly while the molds are face down on them. In this way, the loaves will leave the molds correctly. A *negro* man then places the loaves on one of the canvas cloths covering the separating table. Then one of the *negra* women (known as "mothers of the table") takes a large knife and separates all the poorly refined sugar that has a brown color at the bottom of the loaf. This is called *mascavar*, and this sugar is therefore called *mascavado*. Meanwhile, another slave woman, who has more practice, uses a small ax to remove the wettest part of the *mascavado* sugar, called "the foot of the mold," or *cabucho*. This goes back to the refinery in other molds until it dries. Then, other black women break the lumps of sugar with hammers on top of the canvas cloths. These will also go to the drying tables.

Perfect loaves of sugar have little *mascavado* and yield two and half *arrobas* of white sugar. This is the size of the molds used in Bahia and is a very good yield. If "faces" of sugar for little delicacies are desired, the crater right here and now will use a large knife to cut the top of the loaf in such a way that, once straightened out and made even, it will weigh an *arroba*. After this has been in the sun, it is packed in straw or leather and is shipped to Portugal. Also, if morsels are wanted, the loaf is cut (after removing the *mascavado*) into six or eight pieces and each is made into a square cube, so they may be sent as eye-catching sweets. If small cases or special boxes are wanted, the part of the sugar is selected that matches the wishes of the person who ordered it. The finest sugar from the faces [tops of the loaves] is used to make cases of up to twelve *arrobas,* while thirty or thirty-five *arrobas* are used in a box. From what we have said so far, it will be understood that certain terms refer to different partitions of the sugar. These terms are: box, case, loaf, face, shavings, morsels, lumps, and crumbs. I will reserve for another chapter information about the various qualities and differences of sugar.

Moving now from the separating area to the drying area, as many canvas cloths as needed are brought to dry that day's production of sugar. If the sugar has different owners, it will be noted who owns what by the arrangement of the cloths. If they are continuous in a line, the sugar belongs to the same person. If there are breaks in the line, then the sugar has different owners. What is said about white sugar also applies to the *mascavado*. It is distributed in the same way on its lines of cloths. Once this is completed, the loaves are taken to the cloths. A large straight pole called the "breaking pole," rounded on the hitting end, is used to break the loaf in four pieces. Each of these is quartered again and then again using large knives, and then broken into lumps. Each of these is pounded with hammers into smaller lumps. After it has been in the sun for a while, these are broken into tiny lumps. This method of breaking the sugar is done deliberately. If it contains any moisture, that will be discovered when the loaf is broken bit by bit. For this reason it is not pounded right away into crumbs or powder. Each of the extended cloths is grabbed on the corners and lifted up, making a pile of sugar in each one. At the same time, this allows the boards and the cloths to get warm. Then the piles are raked and, in this manner, the pieces that had been inside are exposed to the sun, and the others at the edges of the cloth are exposed to this new warmth. The slaves continue to stir the sugar, now spread out, with rakes, moving it back and forth. That is, one slave stands on one side and someone else on the other, pushing and pulling the sugar on each of the cloths as they face each other, until the sugar is dry. If during this process they have the bad luck to have a cloud appear that looks like it might bring rain, then they call for help from all the laborers. They will summon even (if necessary) those working at the rollers, stopping the water wheel until all the cloths covered with sugar have been collected and placed in the crating house, or some other covered place. From there, it returns to the drying table on a sunny day when the boards are dry. If the weather cooperates and allows the sugar to dry perfectly, on the same day it can then be moved (in the way that I will explain next), to be weighed and crated following normal practices.

CHAPTER VII

Weighing, Distributing, and Crating the Sugar

FROM THE DRYING counter, the sugar is taken in the canvas cloths to be weighed. The crater is there and ensures that this is done accurately and truthfully so that each gets what is due to him. To make this possible, there are large scales and weights of two *arrobas*, as well as smaller weights and pound weights, which also compensate for the extra weight of the basket holding the sugar. A small spoon is used to remove any extra sugar or add what might be missing to make the exact weight. The two "mothers" assist in the weighing to make room for the crater to weight while seated. Two male slaves move the heavy sugar to the crates, which are dry and carefully prepared. That is, they are plastered with clay inside in the joints, and with a dry banana leaf lining the top of the clay. The crater puts an equal amount of sugar in the crates owned by the planter and in the crates owned by the tenants. Tenants mill their cane at the mill but work their own lands that do not belong to the mill. If the lands belonged to the mill, there would be an additional tax of the *vintena*, or a *quinto*.[6] In addition to half the yield, this would be one loaf from every five, or one of every twenty depending on the local norms. In Pernambuco they pay the fifth and in Bahia they pay the *vintena* or *quindena*, which is one of every fifteen loaves.[7] This depends on what is stipulated in the rental agreement, if the lands are providing income or if they receive less because those lands have not been cleared. Just as the white sugar is weighed and distributed equally, the *mascavado* sugar is also weighed and distributed equally between that belonging to the owner and to tenants whose cane he mills. This leaves only the *mels*. The owner of the mill collects these because of his many expenses. The tax of the tenth owed to God, which is one loaf in ten, is also removed. These loaves remain at the mill and are placed in the crates forwarded by the agent collecting the tax. He sends them empty and removes them when they are filled.

The sugar put into the crates at the beginning is leveled using only a wooden rake or a tamping pole, and there is no pounding to keep from breaking the crates. However, after another two or three weights' worth of sugar have been added, which could be another four to six *arrobas,* it is pounded with eight to ten poles, four or five on each side to keep it even. It is best if the last level of sugar, called "the face of the crate," is made of the finest sugar. It would greatly discredit the mill and be a deception and clear injustice if *batido* sugar were in the middle and white sugar was on top, covering the tainted with the pure and making a liar of the sugar.

Now that the crate has been filled, it is leveled with a wooden rake and a large stick called the *moleque de assentar,*[8] or the "judge." Then it is nailed shut using a drill, hammer, nails, and the clamp iron, to fix any split boards as described above.[9] A crate uses eighty-six nails and is eventually marked in the manner I will explain, indicating the quality of the sugar. We will now turn to that explanation.

Various Types of Sugar Crated Separately, the Marks on the Crates, and Their Transport to the Warehouse

B EFORE MARKING the crates, it is necessary to discuss the various types of sugar that are crated separately, since with this substance also there is a nobility, a base caste, and a mixture. First there are white and *mascavado* sugars. White sugar takes its name from the color it possesses, and it is much admired and esteemed above others. It is remarkable that it absorbs so little color from the clay. *Mascavado* is brown and comes from the bottom of the molds, called the feet or *cabucho*. White sugar can be fine, rounded, or low, and all these are *macho*[10] sugar. Fine sugar is the purest, hardest, and heaviest. Normally it is from the top of the mold. Rounded sugar is a bit less pure, less hard, and ordinarily comes from the second part of the mold. I say "ordinarily" because this is not an infallible rule. Sometimes the top of some molds can turn out less pure and hard than the second part of another mold. Low sugar is even less pure and almost the color of wheat. Although it can be hard and strong, because it is less pure, it is called "low" or inferior.

In addition to these three varieties of white sugar, there is another called white *batido*. It is made from the *mel* from the molds of *macho* sugar in the refinery, cooked, and whisked once more. Sometimes it emerges as pure and strong as the *macho*. There is also *mascavado macho*, which is made from the dregs of the white *macho*, and there is *mascavado batido*, which is the dregs of the white *batido*. That which drips from the molds of *macho* sugar when it is being refined is called *mel*. Drippings from white *batido* are called *remel*.[11] From *mel*, some people make rum by distilling it. Others cook it to make *batido* sugar, and others sell it in pots to those who distill or cook it. It is the same as *remel*.

As we have discussed the various types of sugars, we can now turn to the required marks making the same distinctions on the crates. Crates are marked with hot branding irons or with ink. Each crate needs three marks: the number of *arrobas,* the name of mill, and the planter or merchant sending it. The brand indicating the number of *arrobas* is put at the top of the crate next to the lid. It is made in such a way that the numbers cross the top of the crate and the lid. It is done this way so that, if the crate is opened, it will be obvious, since the markings on the top of the crate will not align with those on the lid.

The sign of the mill is also branded in the same area of the crate, on the right-hand side. This allows for an inquiry if there is a discrepancy in the crating of the sugar. The casks of tar that come from Portugal sometimes have stones in them. The chests of fine cloth sometimes have lengths of burlap inserted in the middle, or the lengths of the bolts are not as long as indicated. Just as these things have happened, they could send fewer *arrobas* of sugar than what was indicated on the crate and substitute *mascavado* sugar in the middle of a crate marked as white. Unscrupulous craters have done this.

The sign of the planter or the merchant sending the sugar, if branded, is placed in the middle of the top of the crate. If it is not branded by fire, it is placed in the same spot in ink. This can be removed with an adze[12] when the crate is sold to another merchant, and the new owner's name can replace it.

If the crate contains white *macho,* it has the mark "B," and if white *batido,* "BB." *Mascavado macho* is "M," and *mascavado batido* is "MB." Each mill has its own mark, such as "S" for the Sergipe do Conde Mill, "P" for Pitanga Mill, and "O" with a cross in the middle for the Jesuit College.

The mills at the shore transport their crates to the port in the following manner: one crate after another is moved with rollers and levers from the crating house to a cart. This cart is specially made for this purpose; it sits a little lower than normal. Each crate is loaded on it and pulled by ropes to the dock by slaves. Their efforts send the crates on their way.

Those mills in the interior transport each crate by an ox cart pulled by three or four pair of oxen, depending on the quantity of mud they must traverse. This process becomes expensive if not undertaken with great care. If the sugar is not transported during the summer, but instead during the winter, it will exhaust and kill the oxen.

From the port, the crates are transported upright on great planks to the ships. Once on board, it is necessary to keep a strong hold on the crates and place them behind the poop deck, so that they do not fall and cause an accident. On the ship, the crates have to be stored with care so that they make the journey safely. Neither too many nor too few crates should be loaded onto the ship, taking into consideration how many it can hold and transport. The vessel should be strong and have many sails and a ship's master who knows the currents and dangers, with sailors who are not groggy from drinking rum. The ship should depart in good weather and high tide.

From the mill to the warehouse or to the departing ship, each crate arriving by sea is charged one *pataca* in freight charges. When entering or leaving the warehouse, each crate is charged half a *pataca*. For the first month, whether it is just beginning or ended, as long as it is not longer than two days, each crate is charged two *vinténs* and one *vintém* for each of the following months. If the manager or crater of the warehouse sells some sugar on commission for its owner, he is paid one *pataca* for each crate.

To this point, we have taken the sugar from the field where it was raised to the ports of Brazil, where it will sail for Portugal. From there it will be divided among the many cities in Europe. Up to this point, a discussion has been lacking regarding the former and current prices for sugar, as well as the reasons why today these are so excessive.

CHAPTER IX

The Past and Present Prices of Sugar

TWENTY YEARS AGO, the prices in these parts changed a lot for white, *mascavado,* and *batido* sugars. The white that was selling for eight, nine, or ten *tostões* per *arroba* afterward rose to twelve, fifteen, and sixteen, and finally eighteen, twenty, twenty-two, and twenty-four *tostões.* It then fell to sixteen. The white *batido* that they had let go for seven or eight *tostões* rose to twelve and fourteen. The *mascavado macho,* which had been worth five *tostões,* sold for ten, eleven, and even more. The *mascavado batido,* whose price had been one *cruzado,* reached six *tostões.*

Need forces one to sell cheap and to "burn" (as they say) the fine sugar. This has cost the slaves, the mill owners, and the tenant farmers, who have been working and spending money. The lack of ships is another reason why sugar does not bring the price it is worth. However, another reason is the rapid rise these days of the price of copper, iron, cloth, and other items that the mills require. This is especially true for the cost of slaves, whom they will not let go for less than one hundred *milréis.* In the past, the best slaves were worth only forty or fifty *milréis.* This is the chief cause of sugar's great rise in price, in addition to having local and national coins, and the discovery of gold mines, which serve to make a few rich and to destroy many.[13] The best mines in Brazil are the ditches and furrows where tobacco is planted.

If we consider the intrinsic value sugar merits because of its inherent good qualities, no other substance is its equal. If everyone knows its sweetness when they consume it, there is no reason that it should not be given its extrinsic value when it is bought and sold. The mill owners, the merchants, and the magistrate for revenue should, by rights, adjust its price. After so many expenses, he (the fiscal magistrate) could allow a respectable profit. Following that, if the prices were reduced on goods coming from Portugal and for slaves coming from Angola and the coast of Guinea to something more moderate, then the price of sugar could also be lowered to ten or twelve *tostões*. Everyone agrees that it is impossible for these excessive prices to continue from one side of the Atlantic and the other without the loss of Brazil.

CHAPTER X

The Number of Crates of Sugar Normally Produced Each Year in Brazil

RIGHT NOW IN THE region of Bahia, there are 146 sugar mills in active production. In addition, there are others in production in the *Recôncavo,* along the shore, and in the interior. These days they are the most lucrative. Those in Pernambuco, since they are smaller, total 246, and in Rio de Janeiro there are 136.

Each year the mills in Bahia produce 14,500 crates of sugar. Of these, 14,000 go to Portugal. That is 8,000 of the *branco macho,* 3,000 of the *mascavado macho,* 1,800 of the *branco batido,* and 1,200 of the *mascavado batido.* Some 500 crates of different qualities remain locally.

In Pernambuco, each year they produce 12,300 crates, of which 12,100 are shipped to Portugal. These are 7,000 of the *branco macho,* 2,600 of the *mascavado macho,* 1,400 of the *branco batido,* and 1,100 of the *mascavado batido.* The locals there use 200 crates of various types.

In Rio de Janeiro, each year they produce 10,220 crates, of which 10,100 are shipped to Portugal. These are 5,600 of the *branco macho,* 2,400 of the *mascavado macho,* 1,200 of the *branco batido,* and 800 of the *mascavado batido.* The local population uses 120 crates of different qualities.

All together, the number of crates of sugar produced each year in Brazil totals some 37,020.

The Cost of a Crate of Sugar of Thirty-Five Arrobas Cleared through the Customs House in Lisbon, and the Value of All Sugar Produced in Brazil Each Year

THE LIST THAT FOLLOWS will clearly and precisely show the cost of one crate of white *macho* sugar weighing thirty-five *arrobas*, produced on any mill in Bahia until it reaches the customs house in Lisbon and is cleared through it. Also clearly shown will be the cost of one crate of *mascavado macho*, one of white *batido*, and one of *mascavado batido*. Following this, there is a summary of the value of all sugar produced annually from the harvests in Bahia, Pernambuco, and Rio de Janeiro.

Costs of one crate of white *macho* sugar weighing thirty-five *arrobas*[14]

For the crate itself at the mill, at least	1$200
For making the crate	$050
For 86 nails for the crate	$320
For the 35 *arrobas* of sugar, at 1$600 (per *arroba*)	56$000
For transporting it to the port	2$000
For transporting the crate from the port to the warehouse	$320
For hoisting the crate into the warehouse	$080
For registering it in the warehouse	$080
For storage for one month in the warehouse	$020
For removing it from the warehouse	$160
For local taxes	$300
For taxes for the fortress protecting the harbor	$080
For freight charges, at 20 percent	11$520
For unloading in Lisbon at the customs house	$200
For hoisting it on the customs wharf	$040

For removing it from the customs wharf and placing it in the warehouse	$060
For storing it in the customs house	$050
For installing the hoops around the crate, for each hoop	$080
For works, deductions, and stamps	$060
For estimates and taxes, at 800 *réis* and 20 percent	5$600
For the *consulado*[15] of 3 percent	$840
For the convoy (escort for shipping) at 140 *réis* per *arroba*	4$900
For *maioria*[16]	$600
TOTAL	84$560

Cost of one crate of *mascavado macho* sugar weighing thirty-five *arrobas*

For the thirty-five *arrobas* of said sugar, at 1$000 (per *arroba*)	35$000
For estimates and taxes, at 450 *réis* and 20 percent	3$150
For the *consulado* of 3 percent	$472
For remaining expenses	22$120
TOTAL	60$742

Cost of one crate of white *batido* sugar weighing thirty-five *arrobas*

For the thirty-five *arrobas* of said sugar, at 1$200 (per *arroba*)	42$000
For estimates and taxes, at 600 *réis* and 20 percent	4$720
For the *consulado* of 3 percent	$648
For remaining expenses	22$120
TOTAL	69$488

Cost of one crate of *mascavado batido* sugar weighing thirty-five *arrobas*

For the thirty-five *arrobas* of said sugar, at $640 *réis* (per *arroba*)	22$400
For estimates and taxes, at 300 *réis* and 20 percent	2$100
For the *consulado* of 3 percent	$315
For remaining expenses	22$120
TOTAL	46$935

Crates of sugar normally produced annually in Bahia and
their values, each weighing thirty-five *arrobas*

For 8,000 crates of white *macho* at 84$560	676,480$000
For 3,000 crates of *mascavado macho* at 60$742	182,226$000
For 1,800 crates of white *batido* at 69$488	125,078$400
For 1,200 crates of *mascavado batido* at 46$935	56,322$000
For 500 crates used locally at 60$200	30,100$000
THIS TOTALS 14,500 CRATES AND HAS A VALUE OF	1,070,206$400

Crates of sugar normally produced annually in Pernambuco
and their values, each weighing thirty-five *arrobas*

For 7,000 crates of white *macho* at 78$420	548,940$000
For 2,600 crates of *mascavado macho* at 54$500	141,700$000
For 1,400 crates of white *batido* at 63$200	88,480$000
For 1,100 crates of *mascavado batido* at 39$800	43,780$000
For 200 crates used locally at 56$200	11,240$000
THIS TOTALS 12,300 CRATES AND HAS A VALUE OF	834,140$000

Crates of sugar normally produced annually in Rio de Janeiro
and their values, each weighing thirty-five *arrobas*

For 5,600 crates of white *macho* at 72$340	405,104$000
For 2,500 crates of *mascavado macho* at 48$220	120,550$000
For 1,200 crates of white *batido* at 59$640	71,568$000
For 800 crates of *mascavado batido* at 34$120	27,296$000
For 120 crates used locally at 52$320	6,278$400
THIS TOTALS 10,220 CRATES AND HAS A VALUE OF	630,796$100

Summary of the value of all sugar

From Bahia, 1,070 *contos*,[17] 206,400 *réis*	1,070,206$400
From Pernambuco, 834 *contos,* 140,000 *réis*	834,140$000
From Rio de Janeiro, 630 *contos,* 796,400 *réis*	630,796$400
THIS TOTALS 2,535 *CONTOS*, 142,800 *RÉIS*	2,535,142$800

The Suffering of Sugar from the Time It Is Born in the Field until It Leaves Brazil

IT IS A UNIQUE aspect noted by those who study nature that plants of the greatest benefit for humanity cannot offer their perfect gifts without first being completely crushed. This can be clearly seen in Europe in the making of cloth, bread, olive oil, and wine. These critical fruits of the earth are buried, thrashed, trampled, and milled before being perfectly transformed from what they are. We see much more of this in the making of sugar from the first moment it is planted until it reaches the dining table and makes its way between the teeth, and lodges in the stomach of those who eat it. Sugar has such a life of so much suffering that those who make it suffer, do so to keep it from gaining the upper hand. The earth, in obeying the universe of the Creator, gave much to the cane so that it could reward the palates of mankind generously with sweetness. These sensations multiply in pleasures and delights. It also plotted against this same cane, with more than one hundred instruments to multiply inflictions and pains on it.

In order to do this, those who plant the cane break it into pieces and bury it, cut in pieces in the earth. However, in a near miracle, these pieces of cane receive the kiss of life. Do they not suffer, those that grow forth with new life and vigor? They have been chewed on and trampled by various animals, beaten by the wind, and finally beheaded and cut by scythes. They leave the field all tied up. How many times they have been sold before leaving the field! They are washed while still captive or in the carts or on the boats in full view of each other, children of the same earth. This is just like convicts being taken in handcuffs to jail or to execution, suffering among themselves with confusion and filled with terror. Once they arrive at the mill, by what force and crushing between the rollers are they forced to yield their strength? With such disdain their emaciated and shredded bodies are thrown into the sea!

With such wickedness the pressed stalks are burned without mercy. Their essence, taken from their veins and bones, is dragged through the mill pipes, abused and hung from the lift, boiled in the cauldrons, and sprinkled by the slaves (as an additional punishment) with leaching ash. It is almost made into mud in the ditch, given to satisfy the pigs and other animals. It comes skimmed from the kettle and is then insulted by the drunkenness of the intoxicated. How many times is it whisked and stirred with the skimmers? How many times, after being strained, is it whisked and moved from boiling pan to boiling pan with each time a hotter fire? Sometimes it is almost burned and sometimes removed from the fire for a while, only to suffer more torments. The beatings grow stronger in the basins, as do the stirrings with spatulas. It is left as if it were dead in the molds, which are taken to the refinery without the sugar ever having any idea of its crime. In the refinery, it weeps, stabbed and wounded, this unsuccessful sweetness. Here, they put clay on its face and for great mockery, even the female slaves, over the dirty clay, do the refining. Its tears flow in as many rivers as the channels that receive them—and there are many; enough to fill deep tanks. Oh silent cruelty! The same tears of the innocent are put to boil and whisked once more in the boiling pans, and the same tears are squeezed from the sugar by the force of the still. When it bemoans its fate, it gets clay over its face and the female slaves cast themselves over it with repeated washings. It leaves this Purgatory and jail in this manner as pure as it is innocent. On a low bench, it is handed to other women for them to cut its feet with knives. These slaves are not satisfied just to cut them. Together with other slaves armed with mallets, they rejoice in smashing these feet into small pieces. From this, it goes to the last of its torments, which is at a larger and higher bench. Here it is exposed to anyone who wants to abuse it. It suffers the furor of all those who have toiled and become weary making it. For that reason, now broken with mallets, cut with knives, crushed with other hammers, dragged with rakes, trampled with no compassion by the feet of the *negros;* the numerous slaves are also its tormentors. These number all those who wish to approach the bench. Finally, it is placed on a scale with great care to determine its weight after being crushed. Its grave torments cannot be listed, and none can contemplate or describe them. I imagined that after being reduced to this sorry state, it would be left alone. However, I see that once entombed in a crate, they are not satisfied to have beat it with rods or hit it in the face with a stick, turning it to dust. The sealed tomb in which it rests is branded with a mark. In this state, sealed and branded, it is subjected to sale and resale, held captive, confiscated, and hauled. If it breaks free from the prisons at the port, it cannot escape the torments from the sea or of exile with taxes and tributes. It is as certain that it will be bought and sold in Christian lands as it will be endangered and taken to Algeria and traded among the Muslims. In spite of this, it remains sweet and a champion over anything bitter. It will give pleasure to the palates of its enemies at banquets, health at the tables of the ill, and great profits to the masters of the mills. It will also provide profits for those who follow close behind it, to merchants who purchase it and take it into exile to ports, and even greater gains to the Royal Treasury in customs houses.

THE SECOND PART

*The Development and Wealth of Brazil
through the Cultivation of Tobacco*

CHAPTER I

How Tobacco Was Developed in Brazil and What Esteem It Has Attained

IF BRAZILIAN SUGAR has become known in all the kingdoms and provinces of Europe, its tobacco has become much more acclaimed throughout the four corners of the earth. Today it is highly desired, and people expend great effort to obtain it by any means. It has been a little more than one hundred years that this leaf began to be cultivated and processed in Bahia. When the first one to plant it realized a modest profit on a few *arrobas* sent with very little expectation with someone returning to Lisbon, it encouraged him to plant more. He did this, not so much because of the greed of a merchant, but because of the requests from his agents and friends, who sold it at a fair but slightly higher price. It then reached the point that his neighbors copied him and ambitiously planted and sent larger quantities. Later, these were joined by many of the people living in the countryside, those from Cachoeira and others from the interior of Bahia.[1] Little by little, tobacco became one of the most highly esteemed products exported today from South America to the Kingdom of Portugal, as well as to other kingdoms and foreign nations. By this luck, a leaf that had been so underappreciated and almost unknown has given, and now gives, a lot of wealth to the residents of Brazil, and unbelievable tax revenues for the treasuries of princes.

Of this we will now speak: 1. Showing how to seed and transplant it; how it is cleaned and collected; how it is processed and cured; how it is rolled and cleared through the Customs House. 2. How it is crushed and given its fragrance; which type is best for chewing; which for the pipe; and which for crushing and if sifted or powdered. 3. Of its moderate use for health and its excessive and addictive uses in quantity, in its place and time. 4. The rolls that normally leave each year from Brazil for Portugal and the value of these in Bahia and in the Kingdom of

Portugal. Of the penalties levied so that it should not be sent or sold without clearing customs and the manner in which it is smuggled in spite of the vigilance of the guards, both within and outside of Portugal. At the end, we will discuss the income from this business and the distribution of tobacco throughout the world. Everything is according to reliable information, which I solicited and which was given to me by the wisest and most experienced in this line of work. What they told me, I now relate.

The Labor of Tobacco, How It Is Seeded, Transplanted, and Weeded, and When to Plant It

ALL THE WORK and cultivation of tobacco, in its correct order, consists of: seeding, transplanting, trimming, topping, picking the leaves, harvesting, stemming, twisting, wrapping, joining, rolling, wrapping in leather, and pressing. All of these we will discuss in the following chapters. Beginning with the plant, place the seeds in a seedbed that is very rich with manure, or in an interior area cleared by burning, where there are lands for this prepared the same year of the seeding. The usual time of year for seeding is during May, June, and July. After the seed has sprouted, some wild grass will also be growing around it. This should be removed carefully, so that through lack of attention, the baby tobacco plants are not removed with the aggressive grass.

Once the plant is more or less one *palma* high, it leaves the garden where it was born for the fenced fields or livestock areas where it will grow. The more manure in this earth, the better. However, if cattle have been in the area for a long time, it will be necessary to remove some of the manure to prevent its fresh strength from burning the plant instead of helping it.

This new land should have plowed furrows in it so that the plants can stand apart and be seen. The distance from one furrow to the next is five *palmas,* and the plants should be two and a half *palmas* from each other to allow them to grow and spread easily without becoming entangled. The plants should be put in holes one *palma* wide and as deep as the hoe. These holes are then filled with soil containing a lot of manure. With daily vigilance and care, the plants should be inspected to see if caterpillars are present. If so, these should be killed right away to keep them from eating the tender plant. In addition to the caterpillar, the plant's normal enemies are ants, aphids, and crickets. When the caterpillar is young, it eats the base of the plant or its roots. When the caterpillar grows, it then eats the leaves. Ants do the same thing. Because of that, they put leaves from manioc or pepper trees in the furrows where ants appear so they will eat those and not the tobacco. If they eat the tobacco, the leaves are ruined. The aphids are a kind of black mosquito, slightly bigger than a flea. They chew holes in the leaves which, when damaged like this, cannot be twisted. When the plant is young, crickets eat it down to ground level. When the plant is larger, they fearlessly eat the leaves.

Once the leaves have grown more, take the topsoil from the seed-beds where they were first planted and place it around the base of the plant. However, in the winter do not press this soil down very hard, because everything is humid. In the summer, pack it down more firmly to protect the plant. The moisture, which is less, gives the plant its first nourishment. Those who plant it do this.

Once the plant is full grown, with eight or nine leaves, depending on how vigorous it is growing, the flower or bud at the top is removed before it sprouts. This process is also called "topping." Since the plant now lacks this bud, it will grow new ones at the base of each leaf. All these have to be discarded (and this is called "debudding"), so that these do not sap nutrients from the leaves. This treatment of the plants should be done every eight days, more frequently if the weeding is also being done, and should continue until the leaves are mature. This occurs when they have yellow spots on them or when the bottoms of the stems are black inside. This is done normally during the fourth month after the plants have been transplanted.

CHAPTER III

How the Tobacco Leaves Are Picked and Cured and How These Are Treated and Made into Coils

THE TOBACCO LEAVES are broken off where the stem meets the stalk. Gathered together and taken inside, they are left in this state for twenty-four hours, more or less. Before they are heated and dried, they are hung by twos by the stem in straw (which is present in the houses where it is treated) or on poles or in another place where the breeze, but not the sun, will catch them. If the sun does shine on them, they will dry out and lose their strength. Once they have dried, which happens after they have been hung for more or less two days, they throw them on the floor and remove most of the stems from the lower parts of the leaves. This is done carefully so as not to tear the leaves, and is called "stemming." Then the best leaves are folded in half to serve as the exterior layer of the coil made from the remaining leaves. The farmer is advised that leaves picked on one day should not be mixed with others, except those picked the following day, so that they will be equally seasoned. If this advice is not followed, some leaves will damage others.

Now that the leaves have been cured and the stems removed, as said above, the leaves are used to make a coil about the thickness of three fingers. In order to accomplish this, they use a wheel and a special crank to keep the coil in one piece, uniform and strong. Behind it is another machine that collects the coil on a pole or within the device, in the manner of a simple rope and not as if it were a chain. Boys work next to the machine, feeding it the leaves to be twisted into a coil.

"Fabbrica del Tabacco," *Il gazzettiere american*, vol. 3,
Leghorn, 1763 (JCB 09534–30). Courtesy of the
John Carter Brown Library at Brown University

CHAPTER IV

How Tobacco Is Cured after Making Coils

N OW THAT THE COIL has been made to the desired length and wrapped around a pole, it is unrolled daily. That is, in the morning and at night laborers unroll the coil and wrap it around another stick in order to keep the tobacco from getting too warm. This process of transferring the tobacco, the twisting and turning, should be done gently so that the coil is well attached. Once the tobacco turns black, this turning should only be done once daily. As the tobacco improves, the number of twistings should diminish until it reaches the point where it can be collected without fear of its spoiling. Normally this process of conditioning takes fifteen to twenty days, depending if the weather has been more or less humid or dry.

Next in line to this is what is called "joining." This is when three coils of tobacco are put on one pole, where they will remain until the time comes for rolling. Meanwhile, these are placed in a storage area with high scaffolding, with channels below it to collect the moisture that drips from the coils for use later when it is time for rolling.

The last treatment in this process is to do the following: mix the moisture collected from the tobacco with anise, basil, and lard. Those who take on a handful of special orders add musk or ambergris if they have these.[2] With sugarcane syrup added (molasses, the thicker the better), the coils of tobacco are now dipped once into this mixture, just before performing the rolling in the following way.

How Tobacco Is Rolled and Encased in Leather and Those Engaged in This Entire Process from Planting until Rolling

I N ORDER TO ROLL the tobacco, fold a cured and sweetened coil in half, to a length of three *palmas,* on top of a thin, lightweight pole. The ends of the pole have four little pieces of wood shaped like a cross. The coils of tobacco are then wrapped around these ends, pulling and keeping the coils tightly together so that there are no empty spaces among the folds. So that the ends are always straight, rather than using the levels that they have, they fill the empty spaces of this tobacco roll with leaves from the coconut palm, so they are tightly wedged into the interior folds.

Now that the roll has been made, it is first covered with the dried leaves from a pineapple plant secured with rope made from plant fiber.[3] Then it is given a leather cover matching the length of the roll. This cover is stitched closed very carefully, and then the owner puts his mark on the outside. In this manner the rolls cross the land in carts and the sea in boats to be cleared through customs before being loaded on ships. Normally each roll weighs eight *arrobas.*[4]

Now I can speak about the people who grow and process tobacco. This business is such that there is something for everyone to do. Both the high and mighty and the common people engage in this business: men, women, overseers, and servants. However, not all these people cited above can perform every job. To plant the seeds and transplant the tobacco, it is necessary to have someone who understands how this work is done. This will ensure that the method, order, and spacing are done correctly, both for the holes for planting as well as the furrows. Digging the holes is best done by those who work with hoes. The boys thrust the plants, roots first, one by one into holes that have already been prepared. The one planting pats down the soil at the base;

this is done with more or less firmness, depending on the humidity. Everyone is busy searching for caterpillars twice a day—that is, once at dawn and again once the sun has set. During the day the caterpillars are underground. The indication of their presence is a leaf damaged during the night. Working the earth with a hoe is a task for adults. Topping the already grown plant—that is, trimming the flower or bud at the stock—is a job for *negro* experts. Trimming the buds—that is, trimming off the other buds that grow between the bottom of the leaf and the stock—is work for children and adults. Picking the leaves is for those who know when it is the right time by the appearance of the stem where it joins the stock. It should be black. Everybody works hanging the leaves from the heights, which is normally done at night. Stemming the tobacco, which is to remove the stems from the leaves, is light work for both adults and children. Twisting the leaves to make a coil is best for a skilled *negro* man, while the person who turns the twisting wheel or crank should be a strong *negro* man. Securing the heads of the coils of tobacco to ensure the roll is round is work for an experienced *negro* man. Boys feed tobacco leaves to the crank and form the outer layer made from the best leaves. The same people who make the outer layer do the rolling. Two *negro* men should roll and unroll the coils of tobacco from one pole to another. One turns the pole and the other unwinds the tobacco coil wrapped around it. Those who turn and change the coils from one pole to another are expert *negro* men, and three are required for each turning. One unwinds the coil, one collects it on the other pole, and the third turns the pole. The joining process, which consists of taking three coils from one pole and putting them together, is a job for the most dexterous *negro* men. Three are needed, sometimes four, because one is not sufficient for turning and two are needed to secure the roll. The final step of rolling is a job for real experts to ensure that the roll is made properly.

The Second and Third Collections of Tobacco Leaves and Their Diverse Qualities for Chewing, Smoking, or Grinding

EVERYTHING STATED up to this point about tobacco, which is called the first collection of leaves, is the same for the second and third collections as for the first. This is if the soil is able to provide these and it is aided by good weather and manure. So, once the first leaves have been collected from the plant, the stalk is cut to less than a *palma* high above ground so that the second leaves will develop. Once they have grown, they should be topped (as stated above), removing the buds and the wild grass from the furrows. They should give the plants the same treatment during the second collection as was done during the first. If the earth is rich, there will be a third collection, and the rolls of tobacco will increase.

The tobacco from the first collection is the best, the strongest, and the longest lasting. It is good for smoking, chewing, and grinding. The weak tobacco is not suitable for chewing and is only good for smoking in a pipe. Those who want to grind it should add the best stems from the leaves after they are completely dried. Ground together with the leaves, these make the tobacco strong and give it a good color. For snuff, the best is from Alagoas in Pernambuco and from the lands around Cachoeira and Capivaras.

CHAPTER VII

How Tobacco Is Ground, Sifted, Powdered, and Perfumed

IN ORDER TO grind tobacco it needs to be very dry. This can be done by the sun, on a brazier,[5] or in copper ovens, paying attention that it is not burned. To prevent this, it needs to be stirred constantly. The mortar to grind it needs to be made of marble and the pestle made of wood. Once ground, it is sifted. Those who are nimble separate it. The largest pieces are pulled out and ground again until reduced to powder. This form of tobacco is what is most in demand and held in the highest regard.

Sifted tobacco is used a lot in Italy and it is made in this way. Take the tobacco already made into snuff and place it in a glazed container. Add a moderate amount of *mel* or juices from the tobacco. If this is very thick, dilute it with a little wine. Afterward, in order to ensure that it is all mixed, stir it well. Once it has all mixed, remove some and roll it between your hands as if you were making little cakes. Now that it is wet, it is pushed through a fine sieve. In this way, the mixture that passes through the tiny holes in the sieve becomes sifted tobacco, similar to fine powder. The mixture that does not pass through the sieve because it is too thick should be rolled, as stated above, between the hands until it will pass through. Then it is dried in the sun without disturbing it, so that it will not clump and lose its granular quality.

After the sifted tobacco is dry, if a fragrance is desired, sprinkle it with scented water or put it in the same container holding a whole vanilla bean or some ambergris, a liquor, or musk. However, snuff cannot be sprinkled with scented water. When that is added, it will clump and will not remain as it was intended to be: loose in powder form.

Ground tobacco from Brazil is shipped pure, simple, and unaltered in any way. For these reasons, it is held in high regard. However, tobacco ground in some places in Europe is sold in such an altered state that it scarcely deserves the name tobacco. Even orange peels are ground in with it!

CHAPTER VIII

The Moderate Use of Tobacco for Health
and the Great Injury Done to the
Health However It Is Used

THOSE WHO ARE excessively fond of tobacco call it "holy herb." There is no praiseworthy description that is not attached to it in order to defend its excessive use, which is worthy of rebuke and careful attention. It would seem that there are men who cannot live without this "fifth element," puffing away at all hours at home and on the streets, chewing its leaves, using snuff wicks, and filling their noses with this powder.[6] This excess one finds not only with sailors and all sorts of laborers both free and slave, who believe that only tobacco offers vigor and strength. Also many nobles, people of leisure, soldiers serving on duty, and not just a few members of the clergy all defend tobacco's excessive use. This is even when it is obviously not for a home remedy but to satisfy an undue and detrimental craving. I, who by no means use it, have heard it said that tobacco smoke inhaled in the morning on a moderately empty stomach dries the humors in the stomach and aids in digestion. It also helps eliminate our wastes, relieves chest pain when suffering with asthmatic flux, and lessens intolerable dental pain.

To chew it is not very healthful, although chewed moderately in the morning on an empty stomach assists in the digestive process. However, its overuse relaxes the stomach. If continued, at a minimum it suppresses the sense of taste, makes the breath heavy, the teeth black, and the lips dirty.

Some use it with a snuff wick pushed into the nose to cleanse the head and divert nasal drops from falling on the gums and causing dental pain. This will relieve pain if done in the morning and evening. One can only suggest to those who use these wicks that they avoid the embarrassment of being seen with them falling from their nasal cavities.

They always have drops of nasal fluid on them. These foul the beard and repulse those who speak with them.

Powdered tobacco is the most commonly used and is certainly the least healthful. This is as much because of the excesses with which it is used, turning the home remedy into a vice. This excessive use blocks the desired positive effects that might have occurred had it been used in moderation. Turning now away from examining these examples of excessive vice, I recall that only two popes, Urban VIII and Innocence X, censored its use in churches. This was caused by the great indecency with which they viewed it. They judged it to be an intolerable abuse, important enough to specifically mention and forbid its use by both secular and ecclesiastical figures, especially. These men had been poor role models, smoking even when singing in choir during holy service, and even more so for being religious figures who should provide good examples of dignified reserve and modesty for all (especially in holy places). Because of this, both popes came to prohibit it under pain of excommunication. The first (Pope Urban VIII), in a papal letter of January 30 of the year 1642, forbade its use in the church, entry hall, and churchyard of Saint Peter's Basilica. The second (Pope Innocence X), in another letter, with the same punishment, on January 8, 1650, forbade it in all the churches in an archbishopric where it had been scandalously introduced. In some more observant religions, they prohibit the public use of tobacco in churches, punished by not being allowed to attend. That is, the guilty party could not be elected nor could he select others for higher offices and other positions of the order.[7]

CHAPTER IX

How Tobacco Is Cleared through the Customs House of Bahia

THE TOBACCO HAS now been treated and rolled and has paid its tax to God, which is one *arroba* for every twenty. (The income from this tax, from one year to another, yields 18,000 *cruzados*. This comes from Cachoeira of Bahia and its neighboring parishes, not counting what is grown in the other parts of the interior of Bahia, in Sergipe del Rei, Cotinguiba, Rio Real, Inhambupe, Montegordo, and Torre. Not counting the income from the tax on sugar and other small tithes, these other towns yield between 10,000 and 12,000 *cruzados*.) The tobacco travels by cart and boat to the city of Bahia, paying its way, until it is stored in its own customs house, from which 25,000 rolls or more are sent to Lisbon from one year to another. These are taxed by agreement with the city (Bahia) at seventy *réis* for each roll. The king takes one-third, and two-thirds are for the fort in the same city, which receives 5,000 *cruzados*.

An additional sum of three *réis* per *arroba* is collected by the city in the same manner already stated, which yields 1,200 *cruzados*.

Of this tobacco, 13,000 *arrobas* are allotted for trade on the Mina Coast of West Africa, which are organized into 5,000 small rolls of three *arrobas* each. These are also subject to the same tax by the city of seventy *réis* for each roll, totaling 1,000 *cruzados*.[8]

These 13,000 *arrobas* are subject to a royal tax of four *vinténs* per *arroba*, paid to the treasury, totaling 3,000 *cruzados*.

Three thousand *arrobas* are sent to Rio de Janeiro each year, and these pay nothing in Bahia but they will be subject to taxation in this same Rio de Janeiro, where they will yield 25,000 *cruzados*, give or take a little; this is what they collect.

And taking into consideration everything said here regarding the clearing of tobacco through customs, tobacco taxes yield 65,200 *cruzados*.

The Cost of One Roll of Tobacco of Eight Arrobas, *Sent from Bahia to the Customs House in Lisbon, with Duties Paid, Ready to Ship*

The roll of tobacco	8$000
The leather encasing it and packaging	1$300
Transport to the port of Cachoeira	$550
Storage in the warehouse in Cachoeira	$040
Transport to Bahia	$080
Unloading fees at the warehouse of the city	$020
Storage in the warehouse	$040
Transport to the scales	$010
Fees for weighing and taking it out, ten *réis* per roll	$010
Fess on weight, three *réis* per *arroba*	$024
Taxes and transport, other costs in Lisbon	2$050
SUM TOTAL, 12,124 *RÉIS*	12$124

Normally each year, 25,000 rolls of tobacco are sent.
    At 12$124, this equals 303 *contos*, 100,000 *réis*.   303,100$000
Normally each year, 2,500 rolls leave from Alagoas
    in Pernambuco, at 16,620 *réis*, since it is of a higher
    quality, equals 41 *contos*, 550,000 *réis*.   41,550$000
ALL THIS TOBACCO TOTALS 344 *CONTOS*,
    650,000 *RÉIS*.   344,650$000

In *cruzados,* it is 861,625 *cruzados.*

The High Regard in Which Brazilian Tobacco Is Held in Europe and Other Parts of the World, and the Great Tax Revenues It Provides the Royal Treasury

FROM WHAT HAS been said so far, it is easy to understand the high regard and value that tobacco has attained, especially that from Brazil. Notwithstanding (as was stated at the beginning), it has been a little longer than one hundred years since it was first planted and processed in Bahia. The first *arrobas* sent to Lisbon each year quickly became a success, stimulated demand, and led to more requests. More and more *arrobas* were sent. Changing from a specialty to a staple crop, today only the thousands of rolls that the fleets take are sufficient to satisfy the appetites of all nations. This is not just in Europe, but also in other parts of the world, where they order it in spite of its high cost. In Lisbon one *libra*[9] of ground tobacco is worth twenty to twenty-four *tostões,* depending on how fine it is. The king receives 2,200,000 *cruzados* from this business each year. Because of the large quantities of tobacco consumed in all the cities and towns, not even today do the rulers of Europe have a business with a higher income.

Proof of this can be found in what Engelgrave stated in the first volume of *Luz Evangélica,* on the fifth Sunday after Pentecost in the first paragraph, quoting the testimony of the historian Barnabé de Rijcke, who is undoubtedly correctly informed.[10] This author states that in the city of London, the main city of Great Britain, populated with more than 800,000 souls, there are more than 7,000 tobacco shops. Given that each one of these does not sell more than a *florin*[11] and a half of tobacco, they will import their daily sales of 10,500 *florins.* Exchanged into Portuguese money, each *florin* is two *tostões.* That is, they import each day tobacco worth 5,250 *cruzados.* Consequently, for what is sold only in London in one year, amounting to 365 days, they import 1,916,250 *cruzados*. What would be the total sold in all of Great Britain, in Flanders, in France, in all of Spain, and in Italy? That is not to speak of other parts of Europe and what goes beyond Europe. This is especially true for the East and West Indies, where they order Brazilian tobacco because it is ideal and better cured. They order more than what can be supplied in order that agents do not fail to supply merchants trying to deliver to nearby regions.

CHAPTER XII

The Penalties for Trafficking in Tobacco
Not Cleared through Customs and Methods
Used to Avoid Taxation

A
NY ILLEGAL DIVERSION of tobacco from any part of Brazil to avoid
the ledgers or registers by which all legal tobacco is taxed carries
as a fine the confiscation of the tobacco and the ship where it is found,
and five years' banishment to Angola for the guilty party. However,
the penalties for gangs of thieves who break these laws in Portugal are
much harsher. In other kingdoms there are so many such serious penalties that each year they are the ruination of many families. The harsher
these penalties, the stronger the evidence regarding how important this
commerce has become and how highly profitable it is for all the rulers.

An even better proof of the value and profit that tobacco provides is
how many, driven by greed, lose their fear of these punishments, expos-
ing themselves to these risks with no thoughts of the danger. They will
be pulled into the same despair as were others knocked down by their
great confidence. For this it would appear there is no lack of means
that are not used to load and unload the hidden goods, in sight of the
same officials who, like Argos with one hundred eyes patrolled, when
they were not also Briareos[12] with one hundred hands to receive. There
are more lips to keep sealed than fish in the sea. To note some of the
methods, I will tell of the efforts in which not just a few were caught.
Some sent tobacco inside artillery pieces, others inside small and large
crates of sugar. Still others made false tops of sugar loaves and covered
these very well with leather to hide tobacco; others used barrels of local
manioc flour, or pitch, or sugar syrup, covering the top with a deceptive
layer of tinplate to hide the tobacco underneath.[13] Others found crates
of clothes useful, made with false bottoms, in order to create spaces to
hide the tobacco. Others put tobacco in cases of wine in plain sight,

next to the flasks of wine. How much tobacco left and continues to go each year in the bottoms of the hulls of ships and in the ceilings of the cabins and galleys? How much lined nooks and crannies of a ship's dark recesses? Someone did not forget to use the hollow spaces inside figures of saints! Nor should we forget ships carpenters who hide tobacco in hollow pieces of lumber, piled with the other wood they normally use. Then there is the tobacco that enters and leaves in the large pouches of leather of those coming and going. They go back and forth from the ships in ports many times carrying tobacco under jackets and tunics. In addition, there is tobacco dragged beneath the little boats and the casks of water and wine made wet by the waves of the sea. We would never finish if we attempted to list all the deceitful smuggling methods inspired by ambition. However risky these may be, and however frequently they are discovered, they lead to unhappy endings. This clearly shows the high regard, the demand, and the lure of profit, even that with risk, that accompany tobacco.

THE THIRD PART

*The Development and Wealth
of Brazil by Gold Mining*

CHAPTER I

The Gold Mines Discovered in Brazil

IT WAS ALWAYS well known that in Brazil there were iron, gold, and silver mines. However, there was always a lack of interest in discovering and exploiting them. The inhabitants were content with the abundant fruit the land provided from its surface, as well as fish caught in the large and delightful rivers. They did not attempt to divert the natural course of these rivers to examine their depths, nor to open up the ground, as other peoples have done, driven by greedy ambition. Perhaps it was the disposition to search for Indians in the interior, something less scrupulous and more practical, which distracted them from mining.

In the town of São Paulo, there is a lot of common stone used for walls and enclosures. This stone, because of its color, weight, and its veins clearly shows that it is not undeserving of the name given it of "iron-stone." There is iron where they quarry it. This also supports the tradition that iron was mined there and found to be of very good quality for the common items that people asked ironsmiths to make. Most recently, in the hills of Ibiraçoiaba, eight days from the town of Sorocaba and twelve from the town of São Paulo, moving daily at a moderate pace, Captain Luís Lopes de Carvalho, was ordered there by Governor Artur de Sá. He went with a foreign foundry-man, extracted iron, and brought ingots from which excellent items were made.

That there are also silver mines there is no doubt, because in the hills of Colunas, forty *legoas*[1] beyond the town of Itu in the district of São Paulo, directly east of Itu, there is certainly a lot of fine silver. There is also silver in the hills of Sabarabuçu. In the hills of Guarumé facing Ceará, the Dutch extracted a quantity of silver, while they were in possession of Pernambuco. In the hills of Itabaiana, there is a story that the grandfather of Captain Belchoir da Fonseca Dória found silver.

Seeking another silver mining area, Lopo de Albuquerque went beyond the São Francisco River, where he died on his fruitless enterprise.

However, leaving aside the iron and silver mines as secondary, we move to the gold mines. These are so many in number and so profitable for those who work them. First, it is certain that on a high knoll three *legoas* from the town of São Paulo, at a place called Jaraguá, they found so much gold that measuring it went from *oitavas* to *libras*.[2] In Paranaíba, also next to the same town, on Ibiturna Mountain, gold was discovered and mined in *oitavas*. For many years, gold was mined in great quantity in Paranaguá and Curitiba. At first it was mined in *oitavas*, then by *libras* that equaled an *arroba*, given that it required a great deal of work. The income had no limit until they left, after *Paulistas*[3] discovered the general mines in Cataguás and those called Caeté and more recent ones on the Rio das Velhas, and in other places discovered by other *Paulistas*. We will now separately discuss each of these.

CHAPTER II

The Gold Mines Called "General"
and Who Discovered Them

I T HAS BEEN just a few years since the general mines of Cataguá were discovered. Arthur de Sá was governing Rio de Janeiro at the time. They say that the first person to discover gold was a mulatto who had been at the mines in Paranaguá and Curitiba. This fellow went into the interior with Paulistas to look for Indians. After they arrived at Tripui Mountain, he went down the mountain to draw water from the creek with a wooden bucket at a stream they today call Ouro Preto. Putting the bucket into the river to get water, he scraped it at the side of the river and noted that inside were some small steel-colored flakes. He did not know what he had found, nor did his companions when he showed them these flakes. They did not appreciate what they had found so easily. They only remembered that at this place there was a metal that was poorly formed and, for that reason, unknown. Once they arrived in Taubaté, they did not forget to inquire what type of metal that was. Without any additional examination, they sold some of it to Miguel de Sousa for half a *pataca* for an *oitava*. This was without the knowledge of what they were selling, nor did the buyer know what he purchased. They resolved to send a sample to the governor in Rio de Janeiro, Artur de Sá. He made some tests and discovered it was very fine gold.

At a distance of half a *legoa* from the creek of Ouro Preto, another mine was found called the mine at the creek of Antonio Dias. From there, proceeding another half-*legoa,* there is the mine of the creek of Father João de Faria. Next to it, a little more than a *legoa* distant, is the mine of the Bueno Creek and the mine of Bento Rodrigues. From there three days' moderate journey, traveling each day until dinner time, there is the mine of the stream of Our Lady of Carmo. It was discovered by João Lopes de Lima, not counting the other mine on the creek of Ibuprianga. All of these were named for their discoverers and all were *Paulistas*.

There is also a resting place on the road to these general mines, eleven or twelve days' journey from the first mines, walking each day at a good speed until three o'clock in the afternoon. This stop is called the Rio das Mortes [River of the Deaths], because some men died there swimming and others were killed by gunshots, fighting among themselves over the division of the wild Indians they brought from the interior. In this river as well as in the creeks that flow from it, and in others that feed into it, gold can be found. This stopover serves as a way station for those traveling to the general mines. There they find the provisions they need, since these days there are traders and merchants there.

I am not talking about the mine in the Itatiaia Range (that is, white gold, which is gold that is not fully formed). It is some eight days' distant from the creek at Ouro Preto, daily moving at a moderate pace until dinnertime. The *Paulistas* do not deal with this, since they have the other mines with fully formed gold, providing a better profit. These general mines, they say, are at the latitude of the Captaincy of Espírito Santo.[4]

CHAPTER III

The Other Gold Mines along the
Rio das Velhas and in Caeté

IN ADDITION TO the general mines of Cataguás, other *Paulistas* discovered additional mines along the river called Velhas. These are located, as they claim, at the latitude of Porto Seguro and Santa Cruz. These are the mines along the stream of Campo, discovered by Master Sergeant Domingos Rodrigues da Fonseca, and at the stream of the Roça dos Penteados. These include the mine of Nossa Senhora do Cabo, which was discovered by the same Master Sergeant Domingos Rodrigues, and the mine of Nossa Senhora de Monserrate on the stream of the Ajudante. The chief mine on the Rio das Velhas is that located at Sabarabuçum, discovered by Lieutenant Manuel Borba Gato. He was from São Paulo and was the first to take possession of it and his territory.

There are additional new mines that are known in the Caeté region, between the general mines and those of the Rio das Velhas. Various people discovered these; among them is one on the stream discovered by Captain Luis do Couto. He came from Bahia to this stopping place with three brothers, all skilled miners. In addition, there were others who discovered mines secretly and said nothing in order to take all the gold themselves and not have to share it with others. These mines were ultimately discovered by Captain Garcia Rodrigues Pais, when he was opening the new road behind the Orgãos Mountain Range in Rio de Janeiro district, where the Paraíba do Sul River crosses it.

The Yield from the Creeks and the Different Qualities of Gold Extracted from Them

F ROM THE GENERAL mines of Cataguás, the best and greatest yield until now has come from the creeks of Ouro Preto, Nossa Senhora do Carmo, and Bento Rodrigues. From these, in a little more than a strip of land five *braças* long, five *arrobas* of gold have been extracted. Also, the Rio das Velhas is abundant in gold, both along its banks as well as along the islands in it. From the river channel a lot of gold has been and continues to be extracted in abundant quantities.

The *Paulistas* consider a creek lucrative if it provides two *oitavas* of gold in each panning. However, there were pannings yielding half an *oitava* and half a *pataca*. There are also pannings worth three, four, five, eight, fifteen, twenty, and thirty *oitavas* and more. This happened more than a few times along the stream of Nossa Senhora do Carmo, the creek of Ouro Preto, and that of Bento Rodrigues, and the Rio das Velhas.

The heaviest pieces taken from the rivers have included one of ninety-five *oitavas* and another of three *libras*, which was divided among three people with an ax. Another one surpassed 150 *oitavas*, a nugget in the shape of an ox tongue. It was sent to the governor of the New Colony of Sacramento; another nugget was found weighing more than six *libras*.

Regarding the different qualities of the gold, the so-called black gold is called this because, before it goes to the fire, on the outside it has a color similar to iron. It is possible to test it by biting; yellow will immediately appear, bright and the color of an egg yolk. This is the finest gold because it has almost twenty-three karats. When the royal stamp is applied on it in the foundry, it causes fissures in the bars as if it would burst apart. Its inner reflections appear like sun's rays. Gold from the Creek of Nossa Senhora do Carmo is smaller and powdery and rivals the value of black gold because it has twenty-two karats. The gold from the Creek of Bento Rodrigues, even though it is larger and easier to see and very yellow, in spite of this is not as perfect as black gold or the gold from Nossa Senhora do Carmo. However, when there is a lot of it, it is twenty-karat gold. The gold from the creeks of Campo and Nossa Senhora de Monserrate is very large and very yellow and is twenty-one and a half karats. Gold from the Rio das Velhas is very fine and can reach twenty-two karats. Finally, the gold from Itatiaia Creek in color is white, like silver, because it is not yet fully formed, as said above. Not much is done with this, even though some say that when it is melted it sometimes becomes better formed and displays a yellow color.

There was one year when from all these mines or streams more than one hundred *arrobas* of gold were extracted. This does not count what was mined or is mined secretly from other streams where, to avoid paying the royal tax, the discoverers did not register their findings. If the royal fifth [*quinto*] reached seventeen and twenty *arrobas*, with so much gold evading taxation, it is clear that the annual amount of gold extracted, without any exaggeration, is greater than one hundred *arrobas*. In the past ten years, more than one thousand *arrobas* of gold have been mined. If in the first few years, the miners did not extract one hundred *arrobas*, they certainly surpassed that figure later. Gold mining continues until the present with the same or higher production, since more people are prospecting. It is only the royal fifth owed to His Majesty than grows notably smaller. This is because it is diverted to other regions in the form of gold dust, or it fails to enter the royal mint, or counterfeit insignia are used with contemptible deceit. Even so, His Majesty has not failed to find great profit from the mint in Rio de Janeiro. The mint buying gold at twelve *tostões* for an *oitava* and minting in two years three million *cruzados* in national and provincial gold coins resulted in an immediate royal profit of 600,000 *cruzados*.

CHAPTER V

The People in the Mines and
Who Mine Gold in the Streams

THE UNQUENCHABLE thirst for gold motivated so many to leave their lands and follow the very rough roads, as they are in Minas, that only with difficulty is it possible to count the number of people who are currently there. Taken all together—those who have been there these past few years, for a long time, and those who have recently moved there—they say that more than thirty thousand souls are working there. Some are prospecting, others supervising mining, others negotiating, selling, and buying not just the necessary goods for life there but also gifts, more than in the ports.

On the fleets each year come masses of Portuguese and foreigners to head for the mines. From the cities and towns, bays and backlands of Brazil come whites, *pardos,*[5] *negros,* and many Indians serving the *Paulistas.* This mixture is composed of all sorts of people: men and women, young boys and old men, rich and poor, nobles and peasants, as well as secular and clerical figures. Religious figures come from diverse institutions, many of which do not have a monastery or house in Brazil.

As far as governing the daily lives of these people, there has not been until the present any constraint or government that is effective. They obey only some laws—that is, those pertaining to rights and shares of the mining areas. Disregarding everything else, there are no agents or justices that enforce or who can address punishments for crimes. These are not a few, and are mainly homicides and thefts. In regard to their spiritual welfare, up until now there have been doubts among the ecclesiastical prelates regarding jurisdiction.

The king had Justice José Vaz Pinto as his superintendent of these mines. After two or three years, he settled in Rio de Janeiro. I assume he is well informed as to what is happening there because of his vast experience. I also assume that he has pinpointed the disarray, its remedies, and the possibilities of their enforcement.

Also assisting in the region of the mines is a royal attorney and a customs officer, who are paid stipends. Until now, there have been places where the royal fifth [*quinto*] is collected in Taubaté, in the town of São Paulo, in Parati, and in Rio de Janeiro. In each of these Customs Houses there is a supervisor, a secretary, and a foundry man. The latter casts the gold into bars and stamps them with the royal sign, showing that the tax of a royal fifth has been paid from this gold.

If there were royal mints in Bahia and in Rio de Janeiro (since these are the two locations where all the gold arrives), His Majesty would collect greater profit than he currently does. This profit would be increased even more if the mints were well supplied with the necessary equipment, and if funds were available for immediate purchase of the gold from the miners.

We now understand that His Majesty has sent a governor and ministers of justice to better administer the mining regions and a regiment of soldiers to impose order.

CHAPTER VI

The Rights or Shares of the Mines

IN ORDER TO AVOID the confusion, chaos, and deaths that took place during the initial discoveries of gold in the creeks, it was decided that the shares of ownership would be determined in the following manner. The one who discovered the mine has first right as its discoverer, and another right as a miner. This is followed by what belongs to the king, and after that to the Head of the Customs House, and the others are distributed in lots. Those called "whole rights" are thirty *braças* square,[6] and these are the type reserved for the king, the customs official, and the discoverer. The others distributed by lot are awarded in proportion to the number of slaves the individual has brought to prospect. This is at the rate of two *braços* square for each slave or Indian he brings to work the mines. In this way, someone who brings fifteen slaves will be awarded one whole right of thirty *braças* square. In order to be eligible for receiving a share, it is necessary to petition the superintendent of shares, to whom you must also give an *oitava* of gold and another *oitava* to his secretary for handling the petition. Sometimes it happens that five hundred petitions are offered, and the superintendent and secretary take one thousand *oitavas*. Not all the miners receive a share, because some fall short in their payments. Because of this, they request other shares when new mines are discovered. The king's share is sold right away to whoever offers the highest price, and anyone else can trade or sell his share. In this way, at each step miners come and go and their success varies. Some miners with only a few *braças* extract a lot of gold, and others with more land find less. There was someone who, for a little more than one thousand *oitavas*, sold his share, from which the purchaser extracted seven *arrobas* of gold. Whatever share one has becomes a chance of good or ill fortune, finding or not finding gold.

CHAPTER VII

*The Great Availability of Equipment and Daily
Necessities in the Mines and the Indifference
about Their Extraordinarily High Prices*

T HE EARTH THAT gives forth gold is barren of all that gives life to
humans. No less sterile are the better parts of the roads into the
region. It is hard to imagine the deprivation suffered by miners at the
beginning of the gold rush caused by the lack of food. Many miners
were found dead clutching an ear of corn. However, when the abundance of gold extracted and the inflated prices paid for all things sent
there became common knowledge, public houses and inns were established right away. Merchants immediately began to send to the mines
the best items that arrived on the ships from the Kingdom of Portugal,
as well as from other places. This included food as well as gifts and
clothing with which to put on airs, in addition to a thousand French
trinkets. All these were sent there. In this way, people from all over
Brazil sent whatever the earth produced and made a profit that was not
just great, but excessive. Since in the mines the only currency was gold
dust, the lowest price asked or paid for anything was in *oitavas* of gold.
At this point, herds of livestock from Paranaguá were sent to the mines,
and to the Rio das Velhas herds were sent from the pastures of Bahia.
Everything else the city dwellers imagined would appeal to the miners,
they sent. This included all types of natural goods and manufactured
products, both foreign and domestic. Even though the prices today are
somewhat lower, I will list here the normal prices of goods sold in the
year 1703. This was compiled by someone who lived in the region for
three years and was done honestly. The list is divided into three types
of goods: foods; clothing, swords, and pistols; and slaves and horses.

PRICES FOR CONSUMABLE GOODS

A head of cattle, eighty *oitavas*

An ox, one hundred *oitavas*

A measure of sixty cobs of corn, thirty *oitavas*

A bushel of manioc flour, forty *oitavas*

Six rolls made from corn flour, three *oitavas*

A dry sausage, three *oitavas*

A ham of eight *libras*, sixteen *oitavas*

A small pastry, one *oitava*

A *libra* of butter from a cow, two *oitavas*

A hen, three or four *oitavas*

Six *libras* of beef, one *oitava*

A local cheese, three or four *oitavas*, depending in its weight

Flamengo (from Flanders) cheese, sixteen *oitavas*

A cheese from the Alentejo (southern Portugal), three or four *oitavas*

A small container of marmalade, three *oitavas*

A container of sweets of four *libras*, sixteen *oitavas*

A portion of the best sugar, 32 *oitavas*

A *libra* of cider, three *oitavas*

A small cask of rum, delivered by a slave, one hundred *oitavas*

A small cask of wine, delivered by a slave, two hundred *oitavas*

A small cask of olive oil, delivered by a slave, two *libras*

Four *oitavas* of scented tobacco in powder, one *oitava*

Six *oitavas* of unscented tobacco, in powder, one *oitava*

A *vara*[7] of rolled tobacco, three *oitavas*.

PRICES FOR CLOTHING, SWORDS, AND PISTOLS

A jacket made from coarse cloth, twelve *oitavas*

A jacket made from fine cloth, twenty *oitavas*

A silk vest, sixteen *oitavas*

Pants made from fine cloth, nine *oitavas*

Silk pants, twelve *oitavas*

A linen shirt, four *oitavas*

Linen underwear, three *oitavas*

A pair of silk stockings, eight *oitavas*

A pair of shoes made from goatskin, five *oitavas*

A fine hat made from beaver, twelve *oitavas*

A hat for daily wear, six *oitavas*

A silk hood, four or five *oitavas*

A cotton hood lined with silk, five *oitavas*

A tortoise shell container for tobacco, six *oitavas*

A silver-plated container for tobacco: if it has eight *oitavas* of silver, it costs ten or twelve; if made in gold, the price depends on the workmanship

A rifle not with silver plating, sixteen *oitavas*

A well-made rifle, silver-plated, twenty-five *oitavas*

A pistol for daily use, ten *oitavas*

A silver-plated pistol, forty *oitavas*

A knife with a well-crafted point, six *oitavas*

A small knife, two *oitavas*

A pair of shears, two *oitavas*

All the trinkets that come from France and other places are sold at whatever prices the buyers will pay.

PRICES FOR SLAVES AND HORSES

A large *negro* man, energetic and who speaks Portuguese, 300 *oitavas*

A young *negro* man, 250 *oitavas*

A small *negro* man, 120 *oitavas*

A well-trained male slave born in Brazil, 500 *oitavas*

An intelligent or trained *mulatto,* 500 *oitavas*

A good male skilled on the trumpet, 500 *oitavas*

A skilled female *mulatta,* 600 *oitavas* or more

A *negra* women skilled as a cook, 350 *oitavas*

A common horse, 100 *oitavas*

A good walking horse, two *libras* of gold

These inflated prices are common in the mines. They are why prices have risen so much for everything, as has occurred in the ports of the cites in Brazil. Many sugar mills lack the slaves they need. The city folk suffer great shortages in foodstuffs, since these goods are taken where they can be sold for greater profit.

CHAPTER VIII

The Different Prices for Gold Sold in Brazil
and the Amounts of Gold Annually
Extracted from the Mines

T HE PRICES FOR GOLD have varied during the past few years, not only because one was better than the other, because it had more karats, but also because of the locations where it was sold. Gold is less expensive in the mines than in the town of São Paulo or Santos, and it is much more expensive in the cities of Rio de Janeiro and Bahia than in the two towns to which I referred. Also it is worth more in bars after paying the royal fifth rather than in powder, because the gold sold in powder leaves the furnace with a lot of fractures. In addition, there is the factor of the tax of the royal fifth — whether it has been paid or not.

An *arroba* of gold dust at the rate paid in Bahia, which is fourteen *tostões* for an *oitava*, would yield 14,336 *cruzados*. After paying the royal fifth, at the rate in Bahia, which is sixteen *tostões* for an *oitava*, this would total 16,384 *cruzados*.

An *arroba* of gold powder at the prices paid in Rio de Janeiro, which is thirteen *tostões* for an *oitava*, totals 13,312 *cruzados*. After the royal fifth has been collected, it would fetch fifteen *tostões* for an *oitava*, or 15,360 *cruzados*.

In this way, extracting more than one hundred *arrobas* of gold annually, at fifteen *tostões* per *oitava*, which is the current price in Bahia and Rio de Janeiro, with the royal fifth taken from it, what will be imported in Portugal will be 1,536,000 *cruzados*. These one hundred *arrobas* are subject to the royal fifth, which is only just, and they yield twenty *arrobas* to His Majesty, which are 307,200 *cruzados*. However, it is certain that each year more than three hundred *arrobas* of gold are mined in Brazil.

With all this, it will not appear incredible that, from time to time, people talk about those who have become wealthy. Those who discovered these named creeks, those more fortunate in making claims, those who sold cattle and *negros* at high prices as well as other goods and items in high demand, or those who planted or bought fields of corn near the mines—they all obtained what others had extracted from the earth. This is not even mentioning the great wealth that Governor Artur de Sá brought with him the two times he returned from the mines to Rio de Janeiro. Nor does this mention those who were able to amass one, two, or three *arrobas* of gold; and this was not just a few people. It is certain that Baltazar de Godói by way of planted fields and open mining pits pulled together twenty *arrobas* of gold. From various streams and by doing business with farmers, trading in slaves, and goods, Francisco de Amaral earned more than fifty *arrobas* of gold. Not much less did Manuel Nunes Viana and Manuel Borba Gato earn. With a lot of lucre did José Góis de Almeida leave for São Paulo, as did Garcia Rodrigues Pais leave on the new road. João Lopes de Lima was able to extract five *arrobas* of gold from his creek. The Panteado brothers earned seven *arrobas* from their mines and dealings. Domingos da Silva Moreira from his businesses and mines obtained five *arrobas*. João de Góis earned five *arrobas*. Amador Bueno da Vega garnered some eight *arrobas* from the river at Ouro Preto, streams, and other places. To mention the last name, leaving aside others who were very fortunate, Tomás Ferreira was able to collect a fortune by bringing herds of cattle from Bahia to the mines, by purchasing many cultivated fields, and employing numerous slaves in the mines and streams. He accumulated more than forty *arrobas* of gold, some of it gold and some of it owed to him in debt. Speaking of collecting debts of gold, there have been those, who in their displeasure, have let loose some slugs of lead. This happens frequently in the mines.

People in a short time also acquired considerable amounts of gold by selling consumable goods such as rum and *garapa*. The Indians and *negros* hide many *oitavas* of gold as they are mining in the creeks. On holy days as well as in the late hours of the day, they mine gold for themselves. The lion's share of this gold, they spend on eating and drinking. Without thinking about it, they give great profits to these merchants in the same way that light rains, without a crashing boom, make the fields fertile. For this reason, even the most wealthy men do not ignore this method of making money from the fruits of the earth. They have *negra* cooks, *mulatta* confectioners,[8] and locally born innkeepers engaged in this lucrative business, ordering everything that this gluttony seeks and craves from the distant ports.

The Obligation to Pay the King, Our Lord, One-Fifth of the Gold Extracted from the Mines in Brazil

T HIS ISSUE CAN BE examined in two ways. That is, by that which pertains to the external laws issued in the laws and ordinances of the Kingdom of Portugal, or by that dealing with what is an internal right and what conscience dictates.[9]

Regarding the first way, these laws are outlined in the *Ordenações*[10] of Portugal, book 2, title 26, paragraph 16, which is "Among the Royal privileges, included are furs and gold, silver, and any other metals."

In title 28 of the same book 2, it is specifically stated that when claims and grants are awarded, these do not apply to furs and mines. "In as much as" (as stated in the law) "in many of the grants made by us, and by our ancestors the kings, some very generous and wide-spread clauses are made. We declare that these grants and the clauses they contain were never intended to be granted to furriers and miners of any kind, except those where they are named and awarded in the grant. Regarding the awarding of these things, no claim or assertion to ownership can be made, since these royal rights have existed since the beginning of recorded time."

The king can therefore pay for and extract metals from the mines. The fruits of these are reserved for him. However, in recognition of the expenses that this requires and wishing to encourage his subjects to seek these mines and to allow them to share in the profits from these, the king agreed, as stated in title 34 of book 2 of the *Ordenações,* that "all the metals that are extracted, after being melted and purified, are subject to the tax of the royal fifth [*quinto*], regardless of all the costs."

In order to ensure that the said fifth was paid, the king ordered these metals melted into bars and stamped, and they could not be sold until the royal fifth was deducted. They could not be sold even outside the

Kingdom of Portugal, under the penalty of the loss of goods and ten years of exile to Brazil. This is stated in title 34, paragraph 5: "He who sells these metals before they have been stamped, or in their natural state before reaching the mint, will lose his goods and be exiled to Brazil for ten years." Up to this point, this has all been from the *Ordenação* [legal text].

The authorities, which are specialists on this subject, both Portuguese as well as those from other nations, agree that mines are a royal right, because of the royal expenses on behalf of the national good. Because of this, they cannot be separated from the king. Among other Portuguese scholars, Pedro Barbosa, *ad. L. Divortio*, paragraph "Si vir ff. soluto matrimonio," *a n. 17 usque ad 21.* Cabedo, second part, decision 55, "de venis metallor." Pegas, *ad Ord. Regni Port,* book 2, title 28, note 24, as well as authors from other kingdoms who cite Lucas da Pena in particular, *L. Quicumque desertum,* column 2, *post principium, Cod. De omni agro deserto,* and Rebuffo, second volume, *ad leges Galliae, title ut beneficia ante vacationem,* article 1, *glossa ult. Post medium,* page 346. In addition to these, refer to Solorzano, *de Indiar. Gubern,* second volume, book 1, chapter 13, note 55, and book 5, chapter 1, note 19, as well as many others, who state that this is the custom of all peoples. "As to this case" (as stated in note 55)," the law of the Romans and later of all people consider metals that are excavated among the regalia and ordain that they properly pertain to the places of the supreme princes."[11]

In this subject matter, it is a good idea also to pay attention to theologians. The first of these would be Father Molina in *De Justit. & Jure,* disp. 54, a man as knowledgeable about law as theology, especially Portuguese law. He says, "Normally, according to civil law, whether it be the common law[12] or that of particular kingdoms, wherever veins of metals are discovered, they are rightly attributed to the prince or the republic to sustain public expenses and the burdens of the republic," wherefore paragraph 16, title 26 of book 2, *Ord. Lusitaniae Regni* states: "Moreover concerning the royal right of furriers and gold and silver mines and any other metals. 'As, indeed, men are led by the hope of gain to seek and discover things which are in the public good, various laws are customarily made, varying with time and places which accord to the discoverers either a part of what is extracted from what was in that place or a reward.' At the end, in the *Ordenação* of Portugal, it states: 'It is ordained and established that, expenses deducted, a fifth part of the metal that is extracted from that place is to be paid to the king.'"[13]

Father Vasquez,[14] in his *Opusculis Moralibus de Restitutione*, chapter 5, paragraph 4, dub. 2,[15] speaking of the Kingdom of Castile, says, "In our kingdom, any minerals or silver, gold or mercury are to be appropriated to the patrimony of the king by 1.6. *Recop.*, title 13.1.4." He says, "But none of the authors I have cited say by what law the king can appropriate to himself all minerals, even those produced on private property. As to this, it seems to me, one should say that, although, according to natural law, minerals belong to the owner of the land itself, this law as to minerals could have been introduced of old: that they belong to the patrimony of the king; indeed, the lands and fields of this kingdom could have been distributed on this condition, that the minerals would nevertheless still be reserved to the king and be counted in his patrimony."

Molina cites the same reason in *De Just. Et Jure*, disp. 56, last paragraph, in these words, "Granted, indeed, that considering only the law of peoples,[16] those things that are found that lack an owner belong to the first to take possession, nevertheless, the civil law could ordain that one who found treasure by chance in another's field is bound, in the internal and the external forum,[17] to give half of it to the owner of the field, and one who found it by searching is bound to give him all of it. Why, indeed, could it not ordain in a similar way that, to sustain the expenses of the republic, treasures which are then found belong entirely to the king, or that he has a certain portion of them? Nor, indeed, is that to ordain something that is against the law of peoples, but reasonably and for cause to prevent the ownership of the treasure that is discovered from being as it would be if only the natural law and the law of peoples were considered, and to provide that it belong to another; to do that which may best serve the republic and cannot be otherwise done, just as certain hunting is illegal, which would be legal if only the law of nature and of peoples were considered, as is shown in disp. 43." For the same reason, the same can be said regarding the mines, even though they may be found on private lands.

If this reasoning is not sufficient, the forceful arguments made by Cardinal de Lugo[18] in *Tractatus de Justitia et Jure,* volume 1, disp. 6, section 10, note 108, show that the king can reserve mines for himself (even when found on private property) by way of demanding taxes, which must be paid. The king can order a part of what is extracted from such a mine to be paid in tax for the general good. He says, "And *de facto,* by human laws, minerals of this sort are usually assigned to the prince, at least as to the larger or smaller part, and, as to the rest, to the finder, which may be done either because lands were initially distributed to individuals in the province according to this law: that minerals are reserved to be disposed of by the prince, as Vasquez says in *de Restitutione,* chapter 4, paragraph 4, dub. 2, note 17, or, indeed, by way of tax, as the prince may impose other taxes for support and public expenses. In addition, no small justification of this mode of taxation is this: that as gold and silver are the most among the most potent strengths of the republic, it is not expedient that the prince himself and the entire republic depend on two or three private persons who alone gather these metals on their lands or hold them in reserve and make use of them at their pleasure."

So, whether mines can be considered as part of the royal patrimony or as proper taxes for the expenses for the public good, it is certain that the king must have what is his, which is one-fifth of the gold production. This should be free of impurities and not subject to any other expenses. What is laid out in the law, referred to above, is correctly ordered. The punishment aside, by its nature the fifth is owed in the same way as any other tax. These are prescribed for the general good or as a payment for part of royal patrimony, which is due from the vassal to his lord.

Someone might feel that the mines in Brazil should be governed differently than those in Portugal because the kings' rights of ownership are more direct and certain in Portugal than in the conquests of Brazil. If the legal origins of this are examined, the same answer will appear rash regarding the conquest of the West Indies awarded to the kings of Castile by Pope Alexander VI. Many learned scholars carefully and thoroughly considered this question. In their treatises, examining the papal bulls and the authority of the pope in making similar awards and the very just motives for doing so, they decided in the end that doubts about this cannot remain, and it cannot be called into question. This is a ruling of Christ's vicar on this earth, legitimately dated and published after careful consideration and great attention, as the subject demanded. It is defended as just, valid, and legal by notable scholars. Thus, Solorzano, *de Indiarum Gubernatione,* volume 1, book 2, chapter 24, n. 41. Avendanho,[19] *in Thesauro Indico,* volume 1, title 1, the whole and principally paragraph 4, n. 17, where it also states that Mascardo[20] in *Tractatus de Judaeis et Infidelibus,* part 1, chapter 14, does not fail to affirm that the authority of the pope to make such grants is on such solid legal ground that to state the opposite seems to have the flavor of heresy. This is also how Avendanho should be interpreted.

He who asks this question about the colony of Brazil deserves the same answer. None can deny that the Portuguese kings have these same titles of ownership of Brazil and other conquests. These were the proofs cited by all these authors, Solorzano and Avendanho and others, who in a scholarly and sound manner proved that the kings of Castile were the legitimate sovereign rulers of the West Indies as stated in the papal bulls from Calixto III, Nicolas V, and Alexander VI. Solorzano states this in chapter 24 from page 344 to page 353 and in all of book 2 of the first volume of *de Indiar. Gubern.* This material forms twenty-five chapters and, in the third book, another eight chapters with exceptional erudition, he proves the absolute justice by which these conquests were acquired and are ruled.

Speaking on the same topic, Solozano, in his second volume, book 5, chapter 1, regarding mines and metals extracted from them, n. 19, says that the Indies, as well as other places, are subject to the royal right, as it is his patrimony and part of his supreme domain. This is regardless of whether the mines are found on public lands or on those of private individuals. This right is never included in grants or awards, even if widely done, if it is not specifically mentioned. To confirm what he says, he cites twenty-four scholars who interpret *de Regalibus, de Metallis et de Jure Fisci* or who explain chapter 1, *Quae sint regalia,* or the second law, *Cod. De Metallar.* It also states in n. 20 that because of the necessary expenses in extracting the metal from mines in these conquests, the kings will be satisfied with one-fifth of the extracted metal, prohibiting its use until stamped with the royal seal, indicating that the fifth has been paid. Since there might be some doubt if this fifth should be in ore as it comes from the earth and if expenses are included with it or not, n. 16, a royal decree of 1504, ruled on both questions in these words: "The royal fifth is refined of impurities and without any deductions for expenses, handed over to our treasurer or receiver," which is the same as stated in the laws of Portugal, title 34 of book 2: "[A]fter it has been smelted and refined, the fifth is paid regardless of other costs."

Solorzano also notes in n. 27 of the same chapter 1 of book 5, that when discussing fruits of the earth, metals should be included, citing João Garcia[21] in *de expensis*, chapter 22, n. 47; Lazarate, *de Gabellis*, chapter 19, n. 59; Barbosa, in the same paragraph, "Si vir, L. Divortio, ff. Soluto matrimonio;" Marquech, *de divisione bonorum*, book 2, chapter 11, n. 23 and following; Cabedo, decis. 81, n. 2, part 2; Gilken,[22] *de expensis metallorum*, in L. *Certum Cod. De rei vendicat*, chapter 5, page 722; Farinac,[23] qua ets, 104, n. 62 and 63; Tusch,[24] verbo Minerae, conclusion 237 et verbo *Praeventio*, where it deals with the fact that whoever owns the mines must always recognize his obligation; Naevius,[25] in System, ad L. 2 *Cod. De Metallar;* Pancirolus *in Thesaur*, book 3, chapter 31, pages 214, 327, and 372; Marsil,[26] singul. 531; Menoch, cons. 798 to n. 16. Consequently, just like the other fruits of the earth, it is subject to the tenth awarded to the kings of Portugal and those of Castile: ut ex L. *Cuncti Cod. De Metallar.*; Butrius et alii in cap. *Prevenit* de decimis; Rebuffus, quaest. 10, n. 23 and 24; and Solorzano in *Indiar Gubern.*, volume 2, book 3, chapter 21, n. 10. Given that kings (as Solorzano says) do not try to collect these tenths from the miners, taking into consideration their costs, they pay him one-fifth of the gold or silver they extract from their mines, which is part of the royal patrimony and something always reserved, as is stated.

Moving now to another issue, in which it is asked if this law to pay the king one-fifth of the gold taken from the mines is demanded by one's conscience. I say that the answer to this question springs from the false imagination of those not paying heed and who are quick to respond. These people note that this law is linked to a penalty of the loss of goods and a punishment of exile for ten years and other punishments listed in the new legal code on the mines in Brazil. They think this is just a penal law and as such it does not have any moral obligation. Not even when confronted with a possible sentence by a judge do the lawbreakers agree with the uniform thoughts of the theologians and moralists writing on laws and especially on penalties.

However, Father Francisco Suárez,[27] in examining this issue at some length (as usual), in book 5 *Legibus,* chapter 13, n. 2, comes to the conclusion that fees and pensions paid to kings and princes for properties and things extracted from these, are natural and royal taxes based on justice. This is because these princes collect income from their own possessions, possessions that contribute to their income. These princes, in turn, lease these to their vassals with the obligation that they must pay these pensions. Even if there is a stiff penalty, without a doubt this cannot be called, nor is it, strictly penal. It is also a legal obligation and moral, as are agreements between parties. In order to give them more backbone, a penalty can be imposed on the parties to make them honor the contracts or promises to do, or pay whatever sum justice demands. As a result, these laws weigh on the conscience to force the payment of these pensions and taxes in whole and without hesitation, deductions, or deceptions. Although they do not ask because it is a reciprocal exchange, the agreement intrinsically includes this obligation, unless there is an agreement stating otherwise. Up to this point, this material comes from Father Suárez, number 4, *loco citato.*

From this most certain fundamental it can be inferred also with certainty that the fifths of gold extracted from the mines in Brazil are due the king in conscience. The law enacted to ensure the collection of these fifths is not just penal in nature, although it does have a penalty linked to it for those who fail to obey it. It is a legal obligation and moral law obligating the parties in conscience, with the threat of justice held before them. The king is the legitimate lord of the mines (as we have proven in this first part of this question), by virtue of his ownership of them with the conquest of Brazil, awarded by the pope and all the other laws mentioned by Solorzano in all of the second book of the first volume of *Indiar. Gubern.* These rights are held by the kings of Portugal as well as those of Castile. The stated mines are part of the royal right and patrimony, just like other goods that provide royal income and expenses for the good of the nation and to protect and maintain the faith. The king reserves to himself all claims and does not award rights to extract gold from the mines except with the stipulation that he who removes the gold must pay one-fifth of it, pure, refined, and regardless of any expenses involved. Being able to postulate this (ignoring other laws) as a just and well-regulated tax, as has been proven with the reasons and by the authority of so many scholars cited above, it is plain to see that this obligation is based on reciprocal justice. This is just as other pacts and promises are agreed to in a fair contract, normally conducted by these parties. Even though the law does not increase the penalties for those who break it, these fifths should always be paid because they are an intrinsic obligation. The penalty is to facilitate the collection of the fifth, which is owed, and not to create a law that is only penal.

"For the addition of a penalty (Suárez says, number 10) does not take away the obligation which the law, put concisely without a penalty, would impose in conscience; there, granted that a penalty is added, the law itself imposes an obligation to pay the tax or to make restitution (if, contrary to justice, it is not paid) absent any condemnation or judgment even though no one is obligated to pay a penalty before a judgment is given according to generally received doctrine concerning penal law."[28] Making the following addition to this statement, he adds that this is a composite law, as if it were made of tax and punishment. The punishment is increased since the tax provides sustenance for the king or it satisfies the natural obligation of vassals to give a just stipend to the king, who works for the common good of the nation. The punishment is ordered to ensure compliance and to punish those who do not follow the law as they should. This is even though the tax or pension is just and sufficient in its intention. The obligation remains in place, and it is correct that the penalties are increased and enforced if there is any guilty action, other than the entire payment of the tax. Just as common and mutually agreed penalties are put in place between two signatories of a legal contract, he who breaks the contract can justly be forced to pay the stated penalty as well as any interest and damages incurred as a result of his actions. He states that the same occurs here in our case, because it is as if a contract were agreed to between the king and the vassals. The king governs and his underlings provide him with tax and pensions. To ensure payment, he can increase the penalty. This does not decrease the strength and obligations made in the contract but rather acts as a new coercion for the underlings to pay what justice demands they should. Up to this point, my source has been Father Suárez, in the stated chapter 13, number 10.

This appears to be sufficient to demonstrate that the fifths of gold taken from the mines of Brazil are justly due to the king our Lord in conscience and before the threat of punishment. This is just and not only a penal law as some have erroneously imagined. I will add, however, additional reasons to build on this statement. The first of these is that this law of fifths (as mentioned by Avendanho, *in Thesauro Indico,* first volume, title 5, chapter 8, n. 43) is completely rational for the reasons stated by Molina, disp. 56, *de Just. et Jure,* last paragraph, which is that it is reasonably stated that the prince should have something more than other individuals from items of exceptional value, as he does with other goods. This is even when it seems better for the public to receive this share. In addition, when there are no relatives to a certain degree of relation, the goods belonging to deceased individuals who die *ab intestato* go to the Royal Treasury. In punishment for some crimes, the king obtains and confiscates the goods of the guilty party. If a relative of the guilty party, even one who is closely related, removes these goods from the treasury, he commits a crime against justice with the obligation to return them. How much more is needed to say when the fifths of gold provide not only sustenance for the king, expenses for the good of the nation, as well as support and expansion of the faith? In addition, the miners keep the bulk of the gold from which the fifth [*quinto*] has been extracted.

The second argument: because King Philip II of Castile, after hearing the opinions of theologians and counselors of India, wrote resolutely to the viceroy of Peru, the Count of Vilar, in the year 1584, stating, "I am able to collect the fifth [*quinto*] from all of it (that is, the gold and silver workings) and those affected by this are obliged in conscience to pay me." This he would not have thought of, something contrary to the opinions of his theologians and advisors, had it not been for the interpretation, as expressed by Avendanho in the stated chapter 8, number 44, confirmed in Portuguese law where it states that (as stated by

Father Rebelo)[29] fifths are due the king before the threat of condemnation or sentence. Avendanho further states that proof that fifths are due in conscience can be cited in more than twenty authors, among which are included Vasquez, Molina, Lugo, Rebelo, Azor, Léssio, Castilho, Fragoso, and another fifteen who all held the same opinion. I would like to quote from some of these in order to better demonstrate the truth and authority of the people who have this opinion.

Vasquez, in *Tract. de Restitutione,* chapter 5, paragraph 4, number 30, says: "I believe that the aforesaid laws are neither founded on a presumption nor are penal laws: and so they are to be observed though no judgment is expected." And in note 29 he cites Covarruvias, Cajetan, and Navarrus, who agree.

Lugo, first volume, *de Justitia et Jure,* disp. 6, sect. 11, n. 131, says, "Indeed, other laws that are not penal may transfer property to the treasury, and therefore appear to be binding in conscience before any judicial judgment."

Molina, in disp. 56, *de Justitia et Jure,* cited earlier, last paragraph says, "in the internal and the external forum."

The third argument: that the tithe from the gold and silver should be paid in the same manner as with other products from the earth, is proven above by the authors cited by Solorzano, volume 2, book 3, chapter 21 n. 10. It is also proven in Father Suárez volume 1, *de Religione,* book 1 "de divino cultu," chapter 34, nn. 3 and 6, and by Father Tancredus, tract 1 *de Religione,* book 2, disp. 11, n. 7, "ex omnium mente." And it is to be inferred from the general disposition in X 3.30.22, where you find the words: "A tenth of all goods are to be paid the ministries of the Church," and in X 3.30.23 and X 3.30.26."[30] The popes have awarded the tithes from Brazil and other conquests to the kings of Portugal because of the costs the kings made and make in these same conquests and for the other reasons stated in papal bulls (which can be made and were made to other kings and princes, because of the reasons and citing the authorities which Solorzano does in such a learned manner, with the same bulls, volume 2 *de Indiar. Gubern,* book 3, chapter 1), these rights were granted and the tithes from the gold and silver mines in Brazil must be paid. These tithes as well as those from other fruits of the earth are due in conscience. The mines belong to the kings. However, in light of the expenses incurred in extracting the metals, the kings do not attempt to collect the tithe. They are satisfied with the pension or tax of the fifth [*quinto*] and thus cannot be called unyielding but rather benign, as was noted by Avendanho in the work cited, number 45, and with Fragoso, first volume, page 265, paragraph *alii addunt.*

As a result of all of this, the statement that the fifths of gold are due to the king in conscience is the true opinion, most solidly argued, and on the most solid footing. This is both because of the intrinsic motives of its fundamentals, especially those mentioned by Father Suárez cited above, as well as the extrinsic motives based on the authority of the scholars mentioned. These are theologians of the first order. This means opinions to the contrary are very questionable, weak, and unfounded. Officials appointed by the king with the duty to collect the fifths and stamp the gold in the foundries in conscience have the serious obligation to loyally perform their jobs well. It is impossible to disguise the great damage done to the royal patrimony when it is defrauded by the guilty actions of such officials stealing a lot of money. They receive a salary from this same king, who is well founded in his expectation that they faithfully perform their jobs. Ita Avendanho, number 48.

This same Avendanho, in number 56, is of the opinion that the law forbidding the use of gold dust as currency is not based on conscience, as is the law obligating the payment of the fifth [*quinto*]. However, this same gold dust is subject to the requirement for payment of the fifth from whoever obtains it in order to satisfy this intrinsic obligation. With this, it is again confirmed what is stated in the law of the fifths. It is a legal obligation as well as penal in nature. It is a legal obligation because it is what the king's justice demands, which are the fifths obligated by conscience. It is penal in the sense that the punishment for those who break this law is not forthcoming from conscience but rather as a result of a judicial sentence. In a word: the fifth [*quinto*] is always owed because of justice, the loss of goods, and exile only *post sententiam.*

CHAPTER X

The Route from the Town of São Paulo to the
General Mines and to the Rio das Velhas

N ORMALLY IT TAKES at least two months for those from São
Paulo to reach the general mines of Cataguás because they do not
travel all day long, but only until midday. If they push themselves, they
might travel until one or two in the afternoon. This gives them time to
eat as well as rest, hunt, or fish, where it is possible, and eat honey or any
other foods. In this manner, they persevere with great effort.

The route they take goes from the town of São Paulo to the Itatiaia
Range, where the path divides in two. One route goes to the mines of
Caeté or the mines of Nossa Senhora do Carmo and Ouro Preto, while
the other path goes to the mines along the Rio das Velhas. The following is the route outlined from one stopping or resting place to another
along the way, with the distances and number of days that are required,
more or less, between them. These are the places where the miners rest,
or if necessary relax, and tend to their needs. These days supplies are
available at these stops.

On the first day, leaving the town of São Paulo, people normally
make their way to the resting spot at Nossa Senhora da Penha because,
as they say, it is the first jump from home and it is not more than two
legoas.

From there, the path goes to the village of Itaquequecetuba, which
takes a day.

From there to the town of Moji takes two days.

From Moji the route goes to Laranjeiras, traveling until dinnertime,
four or five days.

From Laranjeiras to the town of Jacareí takes one day, traveling until
three o'clock.

From Jacareí to the town of Taubaté takes two days, traveling until
dinnertime.

From Taubaté to Pindamonhangaba, the parish of Nossa Senhora da Conceição, takes a day and a half.

It takes five or six days' traveling until dinnertime to go from Pindamonhangaba to the town of Guaratinguetá.

Traveling each day until dinnertime, it takes two days from Guaratinguetá to the port of Guaipacaré, where the fields of Bento Rodrigues are located.

From these fields to the foothills of the mountains of the well-known Amantiqueira Mountains takes three days' traveling until dinnertime. These mountains have five high peaks that seem to be the first impediments the gold has placed in the path to prevent the miners from prospecting.

From here, the path begins to cross to a creek called "Twenty Passes," because it passes by it twenty times as it climbs these mountains. In order to pass over these mountains, it is necessary to unload the pack animals because of the great dangers of the sheer drops along the way. Because of this, it takes two days to get over these mountains and it is only accomplished with great difficulty. In this area, many large and beautiful pine trees are found, which in season provide pine nuts in abundance to sustain the miners, as well as wild boars, macaws, and parrots.

Later, passing another creek called "Thirty Passes," because the path passes by it thirty or more times, it reaches Pinheirinhos. It is called this because it is where the pines begin to grow. Here there are fields of corn, squash, and beans planted by those who discovered the mines and by others wanting to return there. These are the only foods planted in the fields along the way and at stopping places, and if they have more, it will be some potatoes. However, at some resting places, they are raising pigs, hens, and roosters, which are sold at high prices to passers-by. This only causes more hardship to those on the journey. From this originates the saying that all who cross the Amantiqueira Mountains either suspend or bury their consciences there.

From Pinheirinhos, the path goes to the stop of the Green River. This takes eight days more or less, traveling until dinnertime. Here they have fields and sell many foods, and even offer the luxury of sweets.

From there, walking until dinnertime more or less three or four days, you arrive at the well-known Boa Vista ["Beautiful View"], a

Route de São Paulo aux Minas Gerais
& «Caminho Velho» de Rio de Janeiro.

Map of the route from São Paulo to Minas, as well as the old
route from Rio de Janeiro. Planche V from André João Antonil,
Cultura e Opulência do Brasil por suas drogas e minas, translated
and edited by Andrée Mansuy-Diniz Silva, Paris, Institute
des Hautes Études de l'Amérique Latine, 1965.

well-named spot because of what can be seen from it. It looks like a
New World, very festive, with extensive countryside covered with little
streams, some larger than others, and all with trees and bushes extending shade, with a lot of small palms that can be eaten, and honey that is
medicinal and delicious. This countryside is hilly with highs and lows
but altogether gently rolling. It is pleasant to cross this countryside,
since you can always see and contemplate Mount Caxambu, which is
so high that it touches the clouds.

From Boa Vista, the path goes to a resting stop called Ubaí, where
there are also fields, and it is eight days' moderate journey to reach there
traveling until dinnertime.

From Ubaí, in three or four days you reach Ingaí.

From Ingaí, in four or five days you reach the Rio Grande, which when it is full, causes fear from the violence with which it flows. However, it has a lot of fish and places where you can find a man and a canoe. He who wants to cross the river pays three *vinténs*; nearby are also some cultivated fields.

From the Rio Grande it takes five or six days to reach the Rio das Mortes [River of the Deaths]. Those who did these murders called the river by this name. This is the main stopping place where those on the trail find new provisions, since by that time their supplies will be low. In this river and in the creeks and ravines that feed into it, there is a lot of gold, and a lot has been mined and continues to be mined. This is a pleasant spot, where a permanent post could be made, if it were not so far from the sea.

From this resting spot, in six to eight days you reach the farm belonging to Garcia Rodrigues.

From here, in two days you arrive at the Itatiaia Mountains.

From these mountains, the path divides in two. One goes to the general mines and the mine of the Nossa Senhora do Carmo and Ouro Preto. The other goes to the mines along the Rio das Velhas; each is a six-day journey. Here in these mountains, extending as far as the eye can see, are the beginnings of the corn and bean fields that feed the miners and those working with them.

The Old Route from the City of Rio de Janeiro to the General Mines of Cataguás and the Rio das Velhas

I N LESS THAN thirty days, traveling all day, those who leave from Rio de Janeiro can arrive in the region of the general mines. However, rarely can this schedule be maintained because the roads are so much more rugged than the route from São Paulo. The following is an account from someone who traveled this route with Governor Artur de Sá. Leaving the city of Rio de Janeiro on August 23, they traveled to Parati. From Parati they went to Taubaté and from there to Pindamonhangaba. From Pindamonhangaba they went to Guaratinguetá and then to the back country of Garcia Rodrigues. From there, they went to Riberão. From Riberão, moving all day long for eight days, they arrived at the Rio das Velhas on November 29. They stopped along the way for eight days in Parati, eighteen in Taubaté, two in Guaratinguetá, two at the back country of Garcia Rodrigues, and twenty-six days at Riberão, or a total of fifty-six days. Subtracting these from the ninety-nine days from August 23 until November 29, they spent no more than forty-three days on the trail.

CHAPTER XII

The New Route from the City of
Rio de Janeiro to the Mines

LEAVING THE CITY OF Rio de Janeiro by land with people carrying loads and walking as the *Paulistas* do, the first stop is Irajá. The second stop is at the mill of Constable Tomé Correia; the third is at the docks of Nobrega on the Iguaçu River, where there is passage on canoes and rowboats; and the fourth is at a place named for Manuel de Couto.

He who comes by sea and with an easy sailing in one day, can arrive at the port of the parish of Nossa Senhora do Pilar. In one more day, traveling in a canoe going up the Morobaí River or going by land, you arrive by midday at the referred spot of Couto. From there, the path goes to Cachoeira at the foot of the mountains and you can rest at camps. From that point, you begin to climb the mountains, which is two good *legoas*. Coming down from the summit, you can eat at resting places called the Pousos Frios ["Cold Repose"]. At this summit, there is a large flat plain big enough to hold a battalion. On a clear day, it is a beautiful place from which you can see Rio de Janeiro and its entire bay.

From Pousos Frios, the path goes to the first cultivated fields belonging to Captain Marcos da Serra, and from there in two days' journey to the second cleared lands belonging to the lieutenants.

From the lieutenants' clearing, it is a day's trip to Pau Grande, cultivated lands which open the way. From there, you rest in the wild at the foot of a hill called Cabaru.

From this hill, the trail goes to the well-known Paraiba, which can be crossed in canoes. On this side of the river, there is a small store owned by Garcia Rodrigues, and there are plenty of provisions for those making the journey. On the other side of the river is the house belonging to Garcia Rodrigues with vast cultivated fields.

From here, in two days' journey the trail reaches the Paraibuna River. The first of these days, it passes through the back country and

«Caminho Novo»
de Rio de Janeiro aux Mines.

Map of the new route from Rio de Janeiro to Minas.
Planche VI from André João Antonil, *Cultura e
Opulência do Brasil por suas drogas e minas*, translated
and edited by Andrée Mansuy-Diniz Silva,
Paris, Institute des Hautes Études de
l'Amérique Latine, 1965.

by the second it reaches the edge of the river. Here there are cultivated fields, goods, and provisions for those making the trip. This river is not as wild as the Paraiba and can be crossed in canoes.

From the Paraibuna, it is two days' journey to the lands belonging to the assayer Simão Pereira. The resting place on the first of these is in the wild. From the fields of Simão Pereira, the path goes to those of Matias Barbosa, and from there to the farm owned by Antônio de Araújo. From there, it continues to the farmlands of Captain José de Sousa and on to those of the district administrator, Tomé Correia. From these lands, the path goes to some new fields owned by Azevedo and from there to lands belonging to the judge of the customs house, Manuel Correia, and from there to the lands of Manuel de Araújo. During this entire part of the trip, the Paraibuna River is nearby.

From the lands belonging to Manuel de Araújo, the path goes to a smaller cleared area also owned by him.

From this little area, the trail goes to the lands owned by the bishop, and from there to some other lands also owned by him.

From the second lands owned by the bishop, it is a small journey to Borda do Campo, the farmlands owned by Colonel Domingos Rodrigues da Fonseca.

Those going to the Mortes River pass by these lands to those of Alberto Dias, and from those to the lands of Manuel de Araújo, which are called "Ressaca." From there, the trail goes to Ponta do Morro, which is a large camp where they have established many claims and extracted a lot of gold. There is a little small blockhouse with ditches and a moat erected by the *Emboabas* during the first disturbances.[31] From this spot, the trail continues to the Mortes River, which can be reached by dinnertime.

He who follows the Minas Gerais trail from the lands belonging to Manuel de Araújo, which are the Ressaca do Campo, will pass the fields of João da Silva Costa and from there go to the farmlands of Congonhas, next to where the trail goes around at Itatiaia. From there, the path continues to Ouro Preto, where there are many fields. From any of these, it is a short journey to the camp at Ouro Preto, which is in the backlands, where there is gold mining.

This entire journey is a distance of some eighty *legoas* because of the switchbacks that are necessary, caused by the many great hills. From north to south, it is not farther than two degrees of latitude from Rio de Janeiro. Ouro Preto is at twenty-one degrees and the Rio das Velhas must be around twenty, more or less. This entire journey can be completed in ten to twelve days, if the traveler does not carry a lot of baggage.

From the region around Ouro Preto to the Rio das Velhas, it is a journey of five days, resting at farms each night.

The Route from the City of Bahia to the Mines of the Rio das Velhas

LEAVING FROM THE city of Bahia the first stop is at Cachoeira, and from there the road continues to the village of Santo Antonio de João Amaro and from there to Tranqueira. At that point, the road divides and taking the road on the right, it heads to the pastures of Filgueira, located right at the source of the Rãs River. From there, the road passes by the pastures of Coronel Antonio Vieira Lima, and from these pastures it goes to the camp of Matias Cardoso.

However, if you want to follow the road to the left, arriving in Tranqueira, you follow the new and shorter road created by João Gonçalves do Prado. This route goes straight ahead until it reaches the source of the Verde River, and from this source it goes to the camp of Garça, and from there moving upriver you arrive at the camp of Borba and quickly find the general mines of the Rio das Velhas.

Those who follow the road on the right at Tranqueira, after they arrive at the camp of Matias Cardoso, follow along the São Francisco River, moving upstream until they find the confluence of the Rio das Velhas. They will quickly find the mines along it.

Since when making this journey from Bahia, some walk until midday, others until three in the afternoon, and others from sunrise to sunset, I have listed the correct distances in *legoas* for these two routes from Bahia to the mines along the Rio das Velhas. They are as follows:

From the city of Bahia to Cachoeira, twelve *legoas*.
From Cachoeira to the village of João Amaro, twenty-five *legoas*.
From the village of João Amaro to Tranqueira, forty-three *legoas*.
From Tranqueira, taking the right fork, until the camp of Matias Cardoso, fifty-two *legoas*.

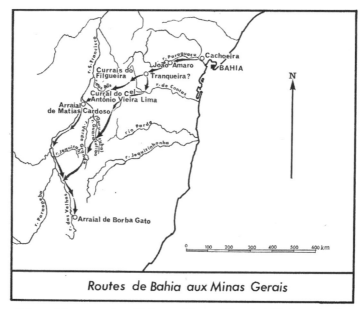

Routes de Bahia aux Minas Gerais

Map of the route from Bahia to Minas. Planche VII from André
João Antonil, *Cultura e Opulência do Brasil por suas drogas e minas*,
translated and edited by Andrée Mansuy-Diniz Silva, Paris,
Institute des Hautes Études de l'Amérique Latine, 1965.

From the camp of Matias Cardoso to the confluence of the Rio das
  Velhas, 54 *legoas*.
From where the Rio das Velhas flows into the São Francisco River
  to the Camp of Borba, where the mines are located, 51 *legoas*. This
  totals 237 *legoas*.
Taking the left fork in Tranqueira, which was a journey from Bahia
  of 80 *legoas*, from Tranqueira to the source of the Guararutiba
  River is 33 *legoas*.
From that source to the last camp on the Rio das Velhas, 46 *legoas*.
From that camp to Borba, 27 *legoas*. This totals 186 *legoas*.

This route from Bahia to the mines is much better than that from
Rio de Janeiro and from the town of São Paulo because it is wider and
easier to travel. It has been opened up by the livestock herds traveling
on it; it has better grazing, and better accommodates the pack animals
and cargoes.

How Gold Is Extracted from the Mines and Creeks in Brazil, as Observed by Someone Traveling with Governor Artur de Sá

I RELATE THE ACCOUNT here that its author sent me, which is the following. This is according to the enterprises, which I personally witnessed in the gold mines of São Paulo. It includes information from both the panning done in the creeks, as well as working the earth next to the mines. I will briefly relate sufficient information so that curious investigators of the natural world can easily tell from their experiences which lands and which creeks can or cannot yield gold. First, in all the mines that I saw and where I was present, I noticed that the land was mountainous, with hills and mountains that touched the clouds. From these flowed creeks filled with water or smaller brooks, all surrounded by groves of trees, both large and small. In all of these creeks, gold is present in smaller or larger quantities. The indication where gold is located is the absence of white sand along the edge of the water but instead the presence of small pebbles and the same kind of stone found at the narrow places in the rivers. The same type of stone can be found underground. Begin by panning at these places; if the mine after some digging shows gold flecks, it is an infallible indicator that the nearby earth also contains gold. By opening the earth with pits and digging the first pit to the depth of ten, twenty, or thirty *palmas,* and after taking out the dirt, which is usually red, you find a type of gravel called *desmonte.*[32] These are little pebbles with sand joined in such a way with the earth that they seem to be something artificial rather than natural. In spite of this, sometimes *desmonte* is found loose and not attached to soil, and it can be bigger or smaller. This *desmonte* is broken up with a crowbar and if by chance it contains gold, it will appear right away, or (as they say) it will sparkle with some flakes of gold in the pan when washed. However, normally if the *desmonte* has a good appearance, this is an indication that the slate rock will have little or no gold. I say "normally" because there is no rule without exception.

Sometimes the *desmonte* can have a depth of more than one *braça*. After it has been removed from the pit, what follows is the crushed rock, which is composed of stones, some of which are large and hard to unearth and so burned it seems they come from a chimney. Once this crushed rock is removed, the shale or slate appears, and it is hard and yields little gold. Around it is mud that is yellow or almost white and very smooth. The whiter it is, the better. Some of this looks like talcum or mica[33] to some, and it serves as a bed for the gold. The hard rock is broken with a mining pick and placed in the pan, as is the soil that was in the crushed rock. This is washed in the river. Little by little, the soil is tossed from the same pan. The water is mixed by swirling and, little by little, the gold (if it is present) will sink to the bottom of the pan. Once all the earth has been washed out of the pan, the gold that remains will show the potential of what the soil will yield.

Some lands have good prospects throughout, while others have it only here and there. All the time, the miners are seeing that pits in one place appear promising while others produce little or nothing. If the earth has a vein, this is the same as a path running through it where gold can be found. The remainder of the pit will reveal little, and miners go after the vein to find gold. This is the best prospecting, where gold is in veins and in quantity. This is an indication that the entire claim where the vein is located will contain gold. The regular pits made in the earth are fifteen, twenty, or more *palmas* squared, and they can be larger or smaller depending on the lay of the land. If at one point the land next to the creek forms a small, flat plateau (because generally the larger areas do not yield as well), this is the best place to work the mine. The usual method of gold mining is to be at the same level as the water. However, I saw many workings (and not the worst ones) that did not follow this rule. Instead, the creek rose up to the mounds, with all the workings as we have stated, of the crushed rock, etc.; but this is not common.

Up to this point, this description has been about the workings at the edge of the creeks. Those miners working in the creeks, if the waterways are able to have water diverted from them, do so by building a

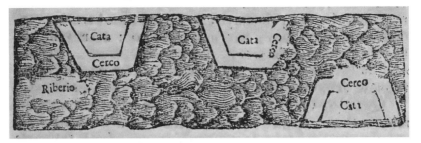

Drawing of mining pits from André João Antonil, *Cultura e Opulência do Brasil*, Lisbon, 1711, p. 171. Courtesy of the John Carter Brown Library at Brown University

structure ringed by a well-aligned wooden wall. The timbers are placed one on top of the other with heavy stakes formed in the shape of a pipe, open from one side to the other so that inside it can fill up with earth (see the accompanying illustration).

This is done when the entire creek cannot be diverted away from its bed. The hills only rarely make this possible. Once the water has been diverted and drained from the pit with pans or gourds, the crushed rock and large and small stones are removed. The water is not very high and the hard slate remains. You examine to see if gold can be found after the pit is worked. Then you move toward the land and open pit after pit. Normally, the pit in the creek is worked first to see if gold is present. If gold is found there, then there will almost always be gold as well on the land in greater or lesser amounts. Many times it happens (as it did in the majority of the workings at Sabarabuçu) that the pit in the water revealed little in the way of gold but the digs outside the water yielded a great deal.

Therefore, to determine if a creek has gold, taking into account the relationship we have explained between the water and the land, make a hole seven or eight *palmas* square and dig until you reach the crushed rock and slate. If there are sparkles, this is an indication that in the water and on land there is gold. By the appearance of these holes, it will be clear if they will yield gold. The pits by the edge of the creek are not worked until these holes are first made. In the creeks where there is sand in the middle and it is absent from the banks, gold can be found if there is also crushed rock. Also, in creeks with sand in between the stones, gold can be found. Emery[34] is found in black sand amid the gold. Wherever emery is found, if the creek has crushed rock, gold will be present.

When the gold runs in veins, normally it runs from the creek into its bed. In the same creek, if you succeed in finding many veins, they will be separated some distance from each other. If a formation is believed to exist near the vein, it is still only in the vein where gold will be found. There are also a lot of pebbles that contain gold flakes.

These are some things that can be said about these mines so that tests can be made in creeks where gold may be present. I will not leave out, with all the other information that I have given, that I saw something that seems impossible by all the norms of mining gold. This was at the famous Rio das Velhas. This occurred on a peninsula that jutted almost halfway into the river and which was covered with water when the river was high. I saw where two little creek beds next to the river were being worked. They had been dug up with crowbars, and the entire beds were filled with hard, light-colored slate. The rock and the creek beds were filled with so much gold that is was obvious even before panning it in the river. They were selling pieces of gold and gold flakes directly from the pan. Once they started panning it, they were finding forty, fifty, and more *oitavas*. The normal yield they obtain in panning is eight or more *oitavas*. Later they worked the soil on this peninsula and each time the yield was less, even though they found all the layers we have mentioned of soil, *desmonte*, crushed rock, and slate. There are no rules without exceptions, as I said. Many times he who prospects a great deal in a pit will find no gold; it will fall to a miner with more luck. Many times they will also find a type of *desmonte* called *tapanhuacanga*. It is worth the same as *cabeça de negro*, because of the composition of the stone. It is so hard that only the force of iron will break it apart. It is also not a bad sign, since many times the crushed rock underneath it will yield gold.

I will not speak about additional details concerning these mines, since they are not as important. I will not discuss them because they are things better seen than described in writing. The details included here are sufficient for those who seek them out of curiosity or who want to understand the workings of a mine.

How to Recognize Silver Mines

FIRST, GENERALLY, silver mines can be found in lands with red or white earth, land without trees and with little grass. You should always look at the top of the knolls and hills, since this is where the veins of silver pop up in the same way that old walls follow straight lines, or how foundations are underground, or how a mountain top is made of many stones piled in a ring. If you find many stones together, always look for the largest or the one that is more or less in the middle of the mound. In prospecting a *vara* or *braça*, always following the vein, experience can be gained of the types of metals present. There are veins that contain five or six types of stone, which Castilians call metals. These veins are usually one *braça*, or four, three, two, or one *palma* wide. Mostly within the vein there is soil of various colors. Sometimes it is all compacted stone and is normally black and white like pebbles. When there is soil between the stone, both it and the stone contain silver. These veins usually occur in wild crags; from the surface of the earth to underneath it, they are always compacted.

The stone is of various colors and distinct. It is vibrant white and black and similar to isinglass[35] used to add sparkle to letters. It is the color of gold, yellow, blue, greenish, brown, the color of liver,[36] orange, and tawny.[37] Normally it has holes in it where the silver forms in lumps. Other stones are filled with silver, while still others have veins of silver in them. In these stones only, they know right away that they contain silver. However, only the most experienced will know or come to possess knowledge of the stones mentioned above. Also, at times a piece of black isinglass is found and is covered in silver. Normally one *libra* of this isinglass will yield two *onças*[38] of silver. For the most part, there are no veins of silver without white or yellow isinglass, rough stones, or earth next to them.

The Castilians call all these stones metals. Some give them these names: *metal cobriço* is a very heavy green stone, salty to the taste and an astringent. It burns the lips with a taste of a mixture of antimony and acid. *Metal polvorilha* is a somewhat yellow stone and is superior to the stone mentioned above. Sometimes deep within it, it yields solid pieces of silver. First-quality *metal negrilho* is a black stone with glimmerings of large pieces of iron, and it is an inferior stone. It is mixed with a black metal of second quality with small, shiny bits of sand, and that of a third quality which is the type that, when powdered, has no shiny qualities. It is the best, and notice should be taken of it. *Metal rosicler*[39] is a black stone similar to the *metal negrilho,* with more sand. It produces a dark powder without any shimmer. In order to determine if it is *rosicler,* pour water over it and use a knife or key as people do when grinding, and it forms a type of mud as if it were bleeding from having been stabbed. The more the mud is stirred, the stronger is the rose coloring. It is a very rich mineral and easy to extract. Where the water flows from the hills, all you need do is look for it. In a mud trough it becomes like clay, and it produces little stones in all the colors.

Metal paco is also like the *rosicler,* and it is a stone that is almost brown, like a brown cloth or something darkened by smoke and very heavy. It would be very complex to list its attributes, qualities, and uses when it forms layers. It is used in a variety of ways depending on the types of *pacos.* However, the stone does not have a good taste when crushed and chewed, but it is a superior stone to use in casting at a foundry because it contains a lot of lead, which helps in casting. The metal and the *negrilho* are the most common found in the mines; their veins do not disappear, nor do they change. Where there is a lot of it, *pacos* stone will shift to *negrilhos* and *negrilhos* to *pacos. Metal plomo ronco* is a stone the color of lead only darker. It is very hard and heavy. It is very plentiful at lower depths. Some state that the Charruas Indians, who live or lived next to the Portuguese at the Colônia do Sacramento, made round balls from it, as a weapon to throw.[40]

How to Recognize Silver and Purify Metals

I F THERE IS kindling (and the best to burn are the droppings from livestock because they create a stronger fire), make a fireplace and in the middle place some of the stones from the mine. Let them burn until they turn red in the way that iron does. Once they are red, throw them into cold water, each in a different place so that you can discern which of the colors has more silver. This will be obvious once they are in the water, since, if a stone has silver, it will sparkle throughout the stone like the heads of pins or little pieces of gunshot.

It is also possible to recognize silver using lead in the following manner. When the ore is black, with few white veins (which, if there are many, use mercury), being very heavy, they are crushed so that the biggest pieces are the size of ground wheat. In a furnace, like a foundry where bells are cast, lead is added. Then the crushed rock is added. Half an *arroba* of lead will treat six *libras* of stone in this manner.

Once the lead has melted and is glowing, throw in two *libras* of stone, placing the stone over the top of the lead. Once the stone has been completely mixed with the lead, continue adding the stone until all six *libras* are mixed. After all the stone or metal has been added, continue feeding the fire under the lead until the fire consumes the lead or turns it into little flakes that rise to the top. Remove these with a skimmer. Strike the sides of the vessel until the silver bursts forth from a bubble on the surface. Before doing anything, thrust at it three or four times as if you were opening and closing your eyes. Do this in the manner of making waves until everything opens and the silver is liquid and motionless. Then, put out the fire and the liquid silver will be a bit hard. Insert the skimmer at one side and move it around to the other in order to remove the silver from the container.

If you want to test using mercury, use metals that are not black. If they are black, first burn them in an oven, moving them back and forth until they release the malady of bitterness that black metal and stone contain. This burning should be done after they have been crushed. If any other metals contain bitterness, these should be burned as well. So, what I have said is that all metals or stone should be crushed and sifted to the size of wheat flour, and the sifter should be made of cloth. It will free the metals from each other. If there are six *libras,* add a handful of salt and mix everything together with water in the same way that someone mixes lime with sand. After it has been thoroughly mixed, make a small pile softened with water so that it absorbs the salt. Leave this as it is now on a board outside in the sun for four or five days. After these days have passed, pull apart the pile and sift the earth very well. On a good linen cloth pour two *onças* of liquid mercury and using the same cloth, hold it above the sifted earth and squeeze it. Kneed it with your hand for an hour. If it is very dry, add water until it obtains the consistency of clay used to make roofing tiles.

After this, make a pile once more and put it in the sun for the same number of days. At the end of this period, if there is silver, it will be shown in the following way. That is, the mercury and the silver will be transformed into white flakes. If this occurs, add more mercury and mix again as before and place it in the sun for the same period. Then make it wet and mix it more. Once this is done, use an open polished gourd to scoop a small amount of this earth, the size of a nut. Wash this with clean water until the sand is cleaned from the gourd to determine if the mercury has adhered to all the silver. If it is still in flakes, add more mercury as done above.

If the mercury has collected all the silver, it will not make flakes in the gourd and everything will be completely mixed. Now clean the entire pile very carefully. Using a new linen cloth, add the mercury and squeeze it over the material. Heat the ball of matter that remains until all the mercury is burned off and the silver will be a liquid. You will then know if the metals will yield silver or not.

If the mercury is cold (which you will know if it is all balled up within itself as if in a little black bag), add more salt or *magistral.*[41] If it is hot (which you can tell by the silver flakes being very black), add wet ash and mix it well, as indicated above. Some say that this mass should be pulled apart and kneaded twice daily for a period of forty days, and that for each *quintal* of stone, add one *almude*[42] of rock salt and ten pounds of mercury in the manner indicated above.

Finally, I would add these general rules. The mines running from north to south are permanent. Gold mines with their openings from east to west and which have white or black pebbles or red clay are good mines. The lack of rock salt near the mountains with the silver mines is a sign that the mines are not permanent. The Castilians call this "rock salt." Only the inspection by those who are experienced will reveal the nature of the metals because there are other types of stone similar to these but which do not contain silver.

The Damage Done to Brazil by Greed
Following the Discovery of Gold in Mines

THERE IS NOTHING so good that it cannot be accompanied by
much evil because of its misuse. Even the most holy commit the
greatest sacrileges. What a wonder that gold is such a beautiful and
precious metal, so useful for human commerce, so worthy of use on
cups and ornaments in churches for divine services. Because of the
unending greed of men, it becomes a constant instrument and cause
of great harm. The news of the many mines in Brazil beckoned men
of all sorts and from all parts, some of wealth and others vagrants. For
those of substance, who found a lot of gold in their open pits, it was the
source of their haughtiness and arrogance, always going around with
private armed guards, primed to start a fight. Fearless of any justice,
they inflict great and flagrant acts of vengeance. The gold lured them
to gamble freely and spend wildly on superficial things, without reflection, purchasing (for example) a *negro* musician for one thousand *cruzados* and a *mulatta* of ill repute for twice that price to continually commit
scandalous sins with her. Vagrants who go to the mines to find gold do
not look in the creeks, but in the hollow reeds, where those who work
in the open pits hide and guard their findings. They use deplorable
treachery and murder most foul. These crimes go unpunished because
in the mining region, justice does not yet have courts or the respect that
it commands elsewhere. In other places there are highly qualified officials supported by numerous soldiers. We can only hope for a solution,
with a governor and officials now going there. Even the bishops and
prelates of several orders, in their high opinions, do not respond to the
censures to reduce their bishoprics and convents of the many clerics and
religious figures who scandalously wander those parts, even apostates
and fugitives. The very best of everything that can be desired makes
its way to the mining region, which was the cause of the sharp increase

in prices of goods. The mill owners and tenants find themselves deeply in debt. Because of the shortage of *negros,* they are unable to tend to sugar or tobacco, as they easily did in the past. These crops were the true mines of Brazil and Portugal. The worst part is that the majority of the gold extracted in the mines leaves for foreign kingdoms as gold dust or coin. A small amount remains in Portugal and cities in Brazil, except what is spent on the necklaces, ornaments, and earrings one sees today heaped on *mulatta* prostitutes and *negra* women, with much greater frequency than on white ladies. There is no prudent person who would not confess that God permitted the discovery of such quantities of gold in order to use it to punish Brazil. In the same way, he is punishing Europeans with iron by so many wars.

THE FOURTH PART

The Development and Wealth of Brazil by the Abundance of Cattle, Leatherworking, and Other Royal Contracts Remaining in This Colony

CHAPTER I

The Great Expanses of Land for
Pastures in Brazil, Filled with Cattle

THE INTERIOR OF Bahia extends along the coast to the mouth of the São Francisco River some 80 *legoas*. Continuing to the mouth of the next river north, which is called Agua Grande, is some 115 *legoas* from Bahia. From Bahia to Centoce it is 130 *legoas;* to Rodelas in the interior, it is 80 *legoas;* to Jacobinas it is 90 *legoas;* and to Tocano it is 50.[1] Because the cattle ranches and corrals are located where there are open spaces and constant sources of water from rivers and lakes, those in Bahia are located along the edges of the São Francisco River, the Rio das Velhas, the Verde River, the Paramirim River, the Jacuípe River, the Ipojuca River, the Inhambupe River, the Itapicuru River, the Real River, the Vaza-Barris River, the Sergipe River, and other rivers. According to information from various people who move around this area, next to these rivers there are currently more than 500 cattle ranches. Just on this side of the São Francisco River there are 106. On the other side, part of Pernambuco, it is certain there are many more. Not just from all these areas and rivers listed do the herds of live-stock come to the city and Bay of Bahia and to the sugar mills. They also come from the Iguaçu River, the Carainhém River, the Corrente River, the Guaraíra River, and the Piauí Grande River, since they are closer; the road comes directly to Bahia, rather than the indirect route to Pernambuco.

So it is obvious that there are many cattle ranches in Bahia; however, there are many more in Pernambuco. The countryside extends 80 *legoas* along the coast from Olinda to the São Francisco River. Continuing from the edge of the São Francisco River to the Iguaçu River, it is some 200 *legoas*. From Olinda heading west to Piauí, the parish of Our Lady of Victory, it is 160 *legoas*. Heading north from Olinda, to Ceará-Mirim,

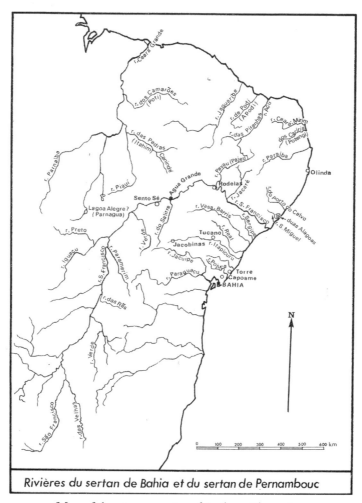

Rivières du sertan de Bahia et du sertan de Pernambouc

Map of the rivers mentioned in the cattle section.
Planche VIII from André João Antonil, *Cultura e Opulência
do Brasil por suas drogas e minas*, translated and edited by
Andrée Mansuy-Diniz Silva, Paris, Institute des
Hautes Études de l'Amérique Latine, 1965.

it is 80 *legoas*. From there to Açu it is 35 *legoas*, and to Ceará Grande it is 80. For all these, they are all almost 200 *legoas* from Olinda.

The rivers of Pernambuco have suitable pastures next to them filled with livestock. (This excludes the Preto River, the Guaraíra River, the Iguaçu River, the Corrente River, the Guariguaê River, the Alegre Lagoon, and the north side of the São Francisco River.) Rivers with livestock next to them include the Cabaços, São Miguel, and the two Alagoas with the river of the port of Calvo, the Rivers Paraíba, Cariris, Açu, Apodi Jaguaribe, Piranhas, Pajeú, Jacaré, Canindé, Parnaíba, Pedras, Camarões, and Piauí.

The cattle ranches in this area must be more than eight hundred, and from all of these come herds for Recife and Olinda and nearby towns. They work in the sugar mills from the São Francisco River to the Grande River, excluding those mentioned above, from Piauí to the banks of the Iguaçu River, and from Parnaguá and the River Preto, because the herds from these rivers almost all come to Bahia. They do this because there is a better road by way of Jacobinas, where they will pass and rest. Others who sometimes come from places even more distant stop there and rest. When they are on the trail and find good pastures, because the rains have come, the herds will arrive in Bahia in less than three months from the most distant ranches. However, if drought forces them to stay in Jacobinas with the cattle, they sell those they brought there. They then rest there six, seven, or eight months, until they come to the city.

On the River Iguaçu alone today there are more than 30,000 head of cattle. In Bahia the number is certainly over half a million, and in Pernambuco there must be 800,000. Bahia receives more of these cattle from Pernambuco, since more herds go there than to Pernambuco.

The area of Brazil with the fewest cattle is Rio de Janeiro, because they have cattle ranches only in the fields of Santa Cruz, some fourteen *legoas* from the city, in the Campos Novos of the São João River, thirty *legoas* distant, and in Goitacases, eighty *legoas* away. In all these fields, the number of cattle does not surpass sixty thousand head that graze there.

In Espírito Santo there are a small number of cattle ranches in Moribeca and a few ranches along this side of the Paraíba do Sul River.

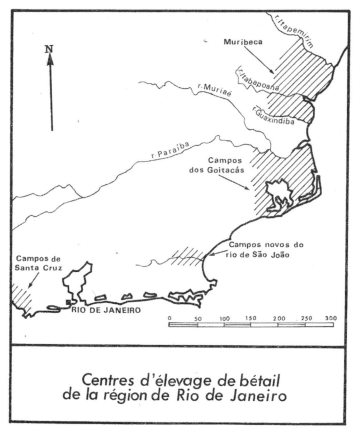

Map of cattle ranches near Rio de Janeiro. Planche IX from
André João Antonil, *Cultura e Opulência do Brasil por suas drogas
e minas*, translated and edited by Andrée Mansuy-Diniz Silva,
Paris, Institute des Hautes Études de l'Amérique Latine, 1965.

The towns in São Paulo kill the cattle they have on their ranches,
which are not very large, and it is only in the fields of Curitiba where
cattle ranching is growing and expanding.

The interior of Bahia is so expansive, as we have mentioned, almost
all of it belongs to two main families of that city, the da Torre family
and the heirs of the deceased colonel Antônio Guedes de Brito. The da
Torre family owns 260 *legoas* along the São Francisco River above it on
the right going to the south and going from that river to the north some

80 *legoas*. The heirs of Colonel Antônio Guedes own from the Chapéus Hill to where the Rio das Velhas begins, 170 *legoas*. On some of these lands, the owners have their own cattle ranches; others are rented, paying ten *milréis* rent annually for the usual size of 1 *legoa*. Thus there are cattle ranches in Bahia and Pernambuco and the other captaincies of 200, 300, 400, 500, 800, and 1,000 head. There are estates owned by those who have such large ranches that surpass 6,000, 8,000, 10,000, 15,000, and more than 20,000 head of cattle. This is where many herds leave each year, depending on favorable or unfavorable weather, the number of calves born, the number of cattle, and the condition of their own pastures as well as those along the trail.

The Herds Normally Conducted from Their Ranches to the Cities, Towns, and Bays of Brazil Destined for Both the Slaughterhouse as well as Sugar Mills, Tobacco Farms, and Other Places of Industry

IN ORDER TO comprehend the number of herds that each year are taken from their ranches in Brazil, it is sufficient to note that all the exported rolls of tobacco leave packed in leather. Each roll weighs 8 *arrobas,* and the rolls from Bahia, as we have noted earlier, annually total at least 25,000 and the rolls from Alagoas in Pernambuco 2,500. It is clear how many head of cattle are needed to pack 27,500 rolls in leather.

In addition to this, each year up to 50,000 half-soles[2] are shipped from Bahia to Portugal, from Pernambuco 40,000, from Rio de Janeiro (I am not sure if these include those from the Nova Colônia do Sacramento or if these are strictly from Rio and the other southern captaincies) up to 20,000, which provides an overall total of 110,000 half-soles.

It is true that not only in the city but also the majority of the better off people residing around the Bay of Bahia sustain themselves on meat on days when meat from the slaughterhouse is not prohibited. It is sold in all the parishes and towns. The *negros,* of which there are many in the cities, commonly live off the entrails, viscera, and intestines, blood, and other innards from cattle. In the high country in the backlands, meat and milk are the usual daily staples for all.

Being that there are so many sugar mills in Brazil, each year oxen are provided for pulling the carts, for the tenants growing sugar, the tobacco farmers, the manioc growers, for the sawmills, and for transporting firewood. From this it can be inferred how many herds are needed annually to achieve this laborious industry. As a result, I will leave this to be considered by he or she who reads this chapter. I think this will be

John Mawes, "Peon Catching Cattle," from *Travels in the Interior of Brazil*, 1823 (JCB 69–02–2). Courtesy of the John Carter Brown Library at Brown University

the wiser course, rather than claiming a precise number of herds. Not even the merchants, which are so numerous and distributed all over the populated regions of Brazil, can state this total with certainty. If I were to state it, I fear no one would believe it but would think it was an extraordinary exaggeration.

Transporting Herds from the Interior, the Normal Prices for Cattle for Slaughter and Cattle for Farmers

THE HERDS THAT usually come to Bahia number 100, 150, 200, and 300 head. Of these, almost every week some arrive in Capoame, a place located some distance of eight *legoas* from the city, where there are pastures and where merchants make their purchases. At some times of the year, there are weeks when herds arrive every day. Those who guide them there are whites, mulattoes, *negros,* and also Indians, who by this work attempt to make some money. Some guide the cattle by singing in front of the herd, and in this way the cattle follow them. Others follow behind the cattle, prodding them and ensuring they do not leave the trail and keep moving. The stages of their journey are four, five, or six *legoas* according to the nature of the pastures where they rest. However, if there is no water, they stay on the trail for fifteen or twenty *legoas* with little rest until they find a place where they can stop. In crossing some rivers, one of those leading the herd places reins on the lead animal, and by swimming indicates where the cattle should cross.

He who wants to entrust his herd to someone to take them, for example from Jacobinas to Capoame, which is a journey of fifteen or sixteen or even seventeen days, pays the guide for his work one *cruzado* for each head in the herd. This pays for the helpers and other guides, and the food for the trip comes from the herd. If by chance the herd numbers two hundred head, the leader receives some additional *cruzados* if they all arrive at their destination. However, if some run away along the journey, *cruzados* are subtracted to match the number of missing cattle. The Indians who come from Jacobinas to Capoame are paid between four and five *milréis.* The man on horseback who leads the herd is paid eight *milréis.* When the distances are greater, the salaries for all are increased proportionately. Thus, coming to Capoame from the Rio São

Francisco and beyond, some who bring herds on their own for others want six or seven *tostões* per head; more if the distance is greater.

A female cow usually sells in Bahia for four or five *milréis*. A male ox sells for seven or eight *milréis*. In Jacobinas, a female cow is sold for two and a half or up to three *milréis*. However, at the cattle ranches in the region of the São Francisco River, where they have a better opportunity to sell cattle for the mines, they sell cattle at their own gate at the same price they are sold in town. Regarding what we have said here about the herds in Bahia, it is more or less the same as with the herds in Pernambuco and Rio de Janeiro.

The Cost of One Hide of Leather and Half a Hide, Treated and Exported from Brazil, Placed in the Lisbon Customs House

Each hide of leather is worth	2$100
Drying it and salting it	$200
Transporting it to the tannery	$040
Tanning it	$600
TOTALING 2,940 *RÉIS*	2$940

A half-hide of leather is worth	1$500
To transport it to the beach	$010
To transport it to a ship	$120
To unload it and take it to the customs house	$010
For the taxes	$340
TOTALING 1,980 *RÉIS*	1$980

The half-hides of leather that normally leave each year from Brazil for Portugal originate from:

Bahia, 50,000 half-hides @1$980	99,000$000
Pernambuco, 40,000 @1$750	70,000$000
From Rio de Janeiro and other southern captaincies, 20,000 @1$640	32,800$000
TOTALING 201 *CONTOS*, 800,000 *RÉIS*, WHICH EQUALS 504,500 *CRUZADOS*	201,800$000

CHAPTER V

Summary of Everything Normally Exported
Annually from Brazil to Portugal and Its Value

As my last demonstration of the wealth Brazil provides for the Kingdom of Portugal, I have now listed here a summary of what I have noted in these four parts of this work. By placing it all together, it will not fail to attract more attention than it did when listed separately.

The value of all sugar	2,535,142$800
The value of tobacco	344,650$000
The value of at least one hundred *arrobas* of gold	614,400$000
The value of leather goods	201,800$000
The value of Brazil wood from Pernambuco	48,000$000
THE GRAND TOTAL, AS CAN BE SEEN, IS 3,743 *CONTOS*, 992,800 *RÉIS*. IN CRUZADOS, THIS IS 9,359,982 *CRUZADOS*.	3,743,992$800

If the income from the whaling contract is added to this total, for six years recently it provided in Bahia 110,000 *cruzados*. In Rio de Janeiro for three years it provided 45,000 *cruzados*. The annual contract for the royal tax collection in Bahia in these past years, not counting the fees, came to nearly 200,000 *cruzados*. In Rio de Janeiro for three years, the total was 190,000 *cruzados,* while in Pernambuco for another three years, it was 97,000 *cruzados*. In São Paulo, it was 60,000 *cruzados,* not counting the other minor captaincies, where the income in each has been markedly growing. The wine contract in Bahia totaled, for six years, 195,000 *cruzados*. In Pernambuco, for three years it totaled 46,000 *cruzados,* while in Rio de Janeiro, for four years, it was more than 50,000 *cruzados*. The salt contract in Bahia totaled, for twelve years, 28,000 *cruzados* each year. The contract for strong liquors both from Brazil and imported, taken together, was 30,000 *cruzados*. Income from the mint in Rio de Janeiro, which in two years has coined three million gold coins, provided the king with its profit. The mint bought gold for twelve *tostões* per *oitava*, provided income of more than 600,000 *cruzados*, not counting the *arrobas* of the *quinto* collected there each year. To this total we should add the taxes paid at the customs houses on the *negros* arriving each year from Angola, São Tomé, and Mina in such large numbers in the ports of Bahia, Recife, and Rio de Janeiro, at the rate of 3,500 *réis* per head. We should also add the 10 percent tax on imports in Rio de Janeiro, which imports each year 80,000 *cruzados*. The continual benefit of Brazil to the Royal Treasury, the ports, and Kingdom of Portugal can be clearly noted. Foreign nations also benefit from the exports from Brazil.

How It Is Only Just that Brazil Is Favored Because of Its Value to the Kingdom of Portugal

B Y WHAT WE HAVE SAID up to now, no one can doubt that Brazil is the best and most productive colony of the many that the Kingdom of Portugal possesses. This is both for the Royal Treasury, as well as for the public good. We have here noted the plethora of goods departing from these ports of Brazil that are true and abundant mines of income. Is there anyone who can doubt that this great and continuous profit justly deserves to attain the favor of His Majesty? Should this favor also not be forthcoming from all his officials in weighing the petitions that Brazilians submit? Should his officials not accept the humbly proposed solutions that benefit and improve the lives of the residents of cities of that state of Brazil? The mill owners, tenants, and tobacco growers are the ones who generate this wondrous wealth. It would seem that they deserve more attention than others in the precedence and consideration of all the courts to promptly hear their cases. These courts can eliminate waiting requirements and thus remove the weariness and the expenses of prolonged legal cases. If the number of residents in Brazil increases so copiously with those from Portugal, each time they populate new regions that were previously empty, they are then very far removed from churches. It is only right that the number of churches is increased, so that everyone has the necessary salvation nearby for his soul. Prompt payment of the soldiers stationed in the outposts and forts in ports will not be forgotten by those affected. If they were treated the same as the soldiers, the governors would not be in their posts. If by his work, his tithes to God increase, then it makes no sense that his qualified sons should be ignored for selection or placement in empty Church positions in the colony. By frequently giving alms to the poor, and being equally generous with the Church, then God should allow prosperity on earth and eternal recompense in Heaven.

The end, praise God

NOTES

Introduction

1. This is suggested by Andrée Mansuy Diniz Silva in Maria Beatriz Nizza da Silva, ed., *Diciónario da História da Colonização Portuguesa no Brasil* (Lisboa: Verbo, 1994), p. 55.

2. Translated and edited by Andrée Mansuy Diniz Silva, published in Paris by the Institut des Hautes Études de l'Amerique Latine.

3. *Manual Bibliográfico de Estudos Brasileiros*, Rubens Borba de Moraes and William Berrien, eds. (Rio de Janeiro: Gráfica Editora Souza, 1949), p. 401.

4. See 3rd ed. (Atlanta, GA: Houghton Mifflin, 1974), pp. 376–82.

5. (Princeton: Princeton University Press, 1983), pp. 55–60.

6. (New York: Alfred A. Knopf, 1966), pp. 89–92.

7. Dauril Alden, *Charles R. Boxer: An Uncommon Life* (Lisboa: Fundação Oriente, 2001).

8. The following were instrumental in my work of understanding and translating the original:

A digital copy of the first edition, available from the website of the Biblioteca Nacional de Brasil.

The 1982 critical edition of the text edited by Fernando Sales, especially his vocabulary of archaic terms used in the text.

H. Brunswick, ed., *Diccionario da Antiga Linguágem Portugueza* (Lisboa: Lusitania Editora, 1910).

Francisco da Silveira Bueno, ed., *Dicionário Escolar da Lingua Portuguesa*. 10 ed. (Rio de Janeiro: Ministério da Educação e Cultura, 1976).

Humberto Leitão and José Vicente Lopes, eds., *Dicionário da Linguagem de Marinha Antiga e Actual* (Lisboa: Centro de Estudos Históricos Ultramarinos, 1963).

Antônio Houaiss and Catherine B. Avery, eds., *The New Appleton Dictionary of the English and Portuguese Languages* (New York: Appleton-Century-Crofts, 1967).

H. Michaelis, *A New Dictionary of the Portuguese and English Languages* (New York: Frederick Ungar Publishing Company, 1932).

The website brasiliana.usp.br/dicionario, which allows access to three invaluable historical dictionaries: Raphael Bluteau, *Vocabulario Portuguez & Latino* (Coimbra: 1712–28); Antonio Moraes e Silva, *Diccionario da lingua portugueza,* 2nd ed. (Lisbon: 1813); and Luiz Maria da Silva Pinto, *Diccionario da Lingua Brasileira* (Ouro Preto, 1832).

The French edition, translated by Andrée Mansuy.

For the sections on sugar: Stuart Schwartz, *Sugar Plantations in the Formation of Brazilian Society: Bahia, 1550–1835* (Cambridge, U.K.: Cambridge University Press, 1985); and Nelson Barbalho, *Dicionário de Açúcar* (Recife: Fundação Joaquim Nabuco, 1984).

For the tobacco section: Timothy Breen, *Tobacco Culture: The Mentality of the Great Tidewater Planters on the Eve of Revolution* (Princeton: Princeton University Press, 1985); J. R. Amaral Lapa, "Un Agricultor Ilustrado do Século XVIII," in *Economia Colonial* (São Paulo: Perspectiva, 1973), pp. 141–230; and The South Carolina State Tobacco Museum in Mullins, South Carolina, and its curator, Mr. Reginold Mcdaniel.

For the gold mining chapters: Waldemar de Almeida Barbosa, *Dicionário Histórico-Geográfico de Minas Gerais* (Belo Horizonte: Saterb, 1968); and Maria Chaves de Mello, *Dicionário Jurídico Português-Inglês, Inglês-Português: Portuguese-English, English-Portuguese Law Dictionary* (Rio de Janeiro: Barrister's Editora, 1984).

Brazil at the Dawn of the Eighteenth Century

To the gentlemen planters

1. José de Anchieta (1534–97) was a Spanish Jesuit and one of the early Jesuit missionaries and authors in sixteenth-century Brazil.

The First Part:
The Agricultural Wealth of Brazil in the Cultivation of Sugar

PREAMBLE

1. The author here is noting the similarity and wordplay between the terms for "mill" (*engenho*) and "ingenious" (*engenhoso*).

2. Smaller mills, not powered by water.

BOOK ONE

1. Called "captive" cane, this is cane from lands leased to tenants with this provision.

2. *Banqueiros* and assistant *banqueiros* are sugar masters in training.

3. *Peças:* slaves.

4. Cassava or manioc is a root vegetable similar to a potato that was a staple food for slaves.

5. A *quintal* (approximately 128 pounds) is an archaic measurement of four *arrobas* (approximately 32 pounds each).

6. A *cruzado* is a gold or silver coin, worth 400 *réis* (old *cruzado*) or 480 *réis* (new *cruzado*).

7. *Saloens* is red soil good for growing some food crops but not good for sugarcane. *Massapé* is good, rich earth suitable for growing sugarcane. It holds moisture and is normally black. *Areiscas* is sandy soil mixed with *saloens*. What this passage says, in effect, is that an inexperienced planter will purchase second-quality soil (*saloens*) thinking it is best (*massapé*), and third-quality soil (*arescias*) thinking it is *saloens*.

8. Saint Anthony, the patron of lost items.

9. A *tarefa* is 30 square *braças* of land, or 4,352 square meters. This equals slightly more than 1 acre.

10. According to the medieval theory of humoral medicine, disease was caused by an imbalance in the four bodily humors: wet, dry, hot, and cold.

11. Communion given by a priest near death.

12. Ceremony wherein a priest forgives a dying person of all sins.

13. That is, living with a women but not being married to her.

14. A service of the church normally said at the third hour of the day—that is, 9:00 a.m.

15. Banns are the public announcements of a pending marriage, normally announced each week for three weeks in a row.

16. Lent is the forty-day period from Ash Wednesday until Easter. Traditionally, it is a period of reflection and prayer, and an observant Roman Catholic would not eat meat during that period.

17. That is, the popes.

18. *Milréis:* one thousand *réis*, written 1$000.

19. A *tarefa* is the amount of sugarcane a slave was obliged to cut in one day, typically 350 bundles each of twelve stalks, or 4,200 stalks of cane.

20. *Claros:* an alcoholic drink made from sugarcane juice.

21. In the sugar-making process, clay is used to cleanse the sugar and make the molds.

22. *Mel* is one of the names for liquid sugar as it is being processed.

23. Called *batido* sugar.

24. Ardas, or Allada, a town and region in modern Benin, conquered by Dahomey in 1724. See James Sweet, *Domingos Álvares, African Healing, and the Intellectual History of the Atlantic World* (Chapel Hill: University of North Carolina Press, 2011), pp. 57–58.

25. São Jorge da Mina, modern Ghana.

26. *Mocambo* in the original, also called a *quilombo:* a community of runaway slaves normally established in the interior away from the plantations. The largest and most famous of these was Palmares.

27. Called *garapa*, a wine made from the dregs of sugar making.

28. Asínio is from the Latin *asinus*: a donkey or a simpleton. Aprício is a reference to Marcus Gavius Apicius, a well-known gourmet of ancient Rome, someone who enjoyed extravagant foods and high society. In other words, this sentence might read, "... it may well be that they have a son devoted to seeking pleasure in the market place."

29. The *tostão* was a coin valued at 100 *réis*.

30. A unit of weight equal to about 32 pounds.

BOOK TWO

1. A large bay and the region around it just south of Salvador.

2. On the west side of the Bay of All Saints, west of Salvador.

3. Sandbars between the sea and the land exposed at low tide.

4. The great bay of Bahia.

5. A *palma* is an archaic measure based on a span (in Portuguese, *palmo*) equivalent to 22 centimeters, or about 8 inches.

6. According to www.proserpine.com/sugar/page8.html, ratoon cropping is "new cane which grows from the stubble left behind after harvesting. This enables the farmers to get three or four crops from these before they have to replant. The reason why the cane does this is [that] sugarcane is a type of grass."

7. A fathom, or *braça*, was approximately 2.2 meters. See Schwartz, *Sugar Plantations*, p. xxiii.

8. Sugarcane was often shipped by river or coastal transport for milling.

9. In other words, five (fingers) times ten (50), times seven (hands) equals 350, times twelve equals 4,200 stalks of cane.

10. *Rodeira:* a type of river or coastal barge used to carry sugarcane or firewood.

11. This is the end of the section translated by Charles Boxer.

12. Emergency water diverter to stop or regulate the turning of the water wheel.

13. *Porca* is a special term for the hole in the beam that holds the main axle of the center roller in the mill.

14. One of the terms for liquid sugar as it is being processed.

15. The typical loaf of sugar in Bahia was two and half *arrobas*, or 80 pounds.

16. A type of palm tree.

17. As noted here, Brazil has a wide variety and range of exotic hardwoods that have many uses. Such woods were an important part of the colonial economy.

18. A silver *tostão* was worth 100 *réis* ($100), a *pataca* 320 *réis* ($320).

19. Yaws is a contagious skin disease in tropical and subtropical regions.

20. Jaguaripe is a town at the far southern end of the Bay of All Saints (Bahia do Todos os Santos).

21. Great iron rods used in making the fire.

22. Here Antonil gives us some very specific information about these copper vessels, and it is clear they were huge. An *arroba* was approximately 32 pounds.

The largest copper vessel he lists here, the cauldrons, at 30 *arrobas* each would have weighed around 960 pounds. The smallest pot used for pouring the liquid into the molds was 128 pounds.

23. The specific term for the female slave who hoists the kettle at the rollers.

24. *Meladura* is one of the names for the liquid form of sugar as it is being processed.

25. Four or five molds for liquid sugar, normally filled at the same time.

26. *Cachaça* is an alcoholic by-product of sugar making.

27. *Calcalha* is the term used for a slave woman working at the skimming kettle.

28. *Garapa* is an alcoholic by-product of sugar making.

29. Candy made from liquid cane.

BOOK THREE

1. A *vintém* (plural *vinténs*) was a coin worth twenty *réis* ($020).

2. *Mascavado* is brown sugar.

3. In English, this is called the intertidal zone, or the foreshore.

4. A *giro* is a wooden platform for drying clay.

5. *Batido* is second-quality sugar.

6. That is, one twentieth or one fifth. The royal tax on precious metals was one-fifth, or a *quinto*.

7. *Vintena* is one twentieth; *quindena* is one fifteenth.

8. Pounding tool used in the crating of sugar.

9. A standard crate of sugar shipped from Brazil at this time weighed thirty-five *arrobas,* or approximately 1,120 pounds.

10. *Macho* is the term for first quality sugar.

11. *Remel* is one of the terms used for liquid sugar as it is being processed.

12. A carpenter's or woodworker's tool used for shaping or shaving wood.

13. Numerous deposits of gold were discovered in the interior of Brazil in the modern state of Minas Gerais beginning around 1689. As a result, the demand for slaves and goods from both the miners and the sugar planters caused prices to rise. This inflationary spiral is one of the core issues addressed directly and indirectly by Antonil.

14. Approximately 1,120 pounds.

15. A tax on goods.

16. A tax.

17. *A conto* is one thousand, hence in this amount it is one thousand and seventy thousands, or 1,070,000.

The Second Part:
The Development and Wealth of Brazil through the Cultivation of Tobacco

1. Cachoeira is a town about fifty miles to the northwest of Salvador de Bahia; it is the highest navigable point on the Paraguaçu River, which empties into the Bay of All Saints.

2. Musk is a scent extracted from deer or similar animals. Ambergris is a waxy substance produced in the intestines of sperm whales. It is found at sea or on the beaches in tropical waters, and was used as an ingredient for perfumes, drugs, and special foods.

3. The text states that they use leaves from the *caravatá* plant (gravatá), *Bromelia pinguin L.*, a pineapple-like plant.

4. Eight *arrobas* is equal to approximately 256 pounds.

5. A brazier is a metal container used outdoors for cooking or heating.

6. By "fifth element" the author probably means that these tobacco users give it equal importance with the four classical elements of earth, water, fire, and air.

7. This passage by Antonil is not clear. By "other religions" it sounds as if he may be referring to Protestants or Jews, which would be the only non-Catholic groups with which he would be familiar. He then uses the word "order," which makes it sound as if he were discussing other Catholic orders besides his own (the Jesuits).

8. The reader must assume here that the author is giving a rough estimate, since 13,000 *arrobas* divided by three equals 4,333 rolls of three *arrobas* each, not 5,000. These 5,000 rolls of tobacco would yield the city 875 *cruzados* at seventy *réis* each, not 1,000 *cruzados*.

9. One *libra* is sixteen ounces, or 453 grams.

10. Henricus Engelgrave, who lived from 1610 to 1670, wrote several religious texts including this one, published in 1648. He was a famous Jesuit preacher and author.

11. A former British coin worth two shillings.

12. Argos: "A giant with 100 eyes, set to guard the heifer Io: his eyes were transferred after his death to the peacock's tail," from dictionary.com. Braireos was one of three ancient storm giants with a hundred hands and fifty heads apiece. Briareos was more specifically a god of sea storms. From www.theoi .com/Titan/HekatonkheirBriareos.html.

13. Tinplate is iron covered in tin.

The Third Part:
The Development and Wealth of Brazil by Gold Mining

1. A *legoa* is an archaic measurement of distance between 2.7 and 3.8 miles, or 5.5 to 6 kilometers.

2. An *oitava* is an eighth of an ounce (3.5 grams); a *libra* is one pound of sixteen ounces.

3. A *Paulista* is someone from São Paulo.

4. That is, farther north, at the latitude of coastal Vitoria, but situated well into the interior of the country.

5. A person of mixed race, usually European and Amerindian.

6. Approximately 21 by 21 feet.

7. A *vara* is an archaic unit of length, about 43 inches, or slightly more than 1 meter.

8. Someone who makes cakes and other sweets.

9. Special thanks to Professor James Gordley of Tulane University for translating the Latin passages in this chapter.

10. Printed collection of laws. More specifically, this refers to the *Ordenações Filipinas,* published in 1603–5.

11. According to the research conducted by Mansuy for the French translation, the legal scholars noted here by Antonil are: Pedro Barbosa (died in 1606), author of *De Matrimonio et pluribus aliis materiebus in titulo ff. Soluto Matrimonio* (published in 1595); Jorge de Cabedo (1549–1604); Manuel Pegas (1635–96), author of *Commentaria ad Ordinationes Regni Portugalliae* (1684); Lucas de Pena (1310?–90?); Pierre Rebuffe and his *Secundus tomus . . .* (1576); and Juan de Solorzano (1575–1653?), author of *Disputationum de Indiraum jure sive De justa . . .* (1639). Virtually all the scholars cited in this section published their legal or theological works in the period from 1500 to 1680.

12. That is, the Roman law as found in Justinian's compilation of legal texts, known as the *Corpus iuris civilis,* which had been recognized as the "common law" (*ius commune*) of much of Europe.

13. Father Luís de Molina (1536–1600) was the author of the six-volume work cited here, *De justitia et jure.*

14. Father Gabriel Vasquez lived from 1549 to 1604.

15. Dub: an abbreviation of the Latin term *dubitante,* meaning "doubting." The term is used in reference to a judge who expresses doubt but does not dissent from a decision reached by the court.

16. The law of peoples (*ius gentium*), sometimes translated as the "law of nations," was a law founded on reason and therefore in force among all peoples.

17. That is, both by the enacted law enforceable in courts and by conscience.

18. Cardinal Juan de Lugo, who lived from 1583 to 1660.

19. Diego Avendanho lived from 1596 to 1688.

20. Josephus Mascardus died in 1588.

21. João Garcia Saavedra.

22. Petrus Gilkenius.

23. Prospero Farinacci lived from 1554 to 1613.

24. Dominicus Tuscus de Regio lived from 1530 to 1620.

25. Sebastian Naevius lived from 1563 to 1643.

26. Ippolito de Marsilo lived from 1450 to 1529.

27. Father Francisco Suárez, S.J., lived from 1548 to 1617.

28. According to the canon law doctrine that Suárez is describing, a person is obligated to make restitution of what he owes to another as a matter of justice even before a court has determined that he has this obligation, but he is not obligated to pay a penalty that the law prescribes for a crime he has committed before a court has imposed it.

29. Father Fernão Rebelo, S.J., lived from 1546 to 1608.

30. The citations are to the Decretals of Pope Gregory IX, also called the *Liber extra* or "extra book." It was a collection of papal decisions that was one of the chief authorities in canon law. The citation form has been modernized. X stands for *Liber extra* and is followed by the number of the book, title, and capitulum.

31. Antonil is referring here to the brief war that took place between the *Emboabas*, or newcomers, and the *Paulistas* who discovered the gold. The conflict began around 1706 and would have been quite recent when he wrote this work.

32. *Desmonte* is gravel and sand fused together.

33. Mica is a mineral that sometimes appears in very thin and transparent flakes.

34. Emery is a hard black or gray stone used as an abrasive.

35. Isinglass is a form of mica, translucent to clear.

36. Dark red.

37. Tawny is yellowish-brown.

38. An *onça* is 8 *oitavas*, or 28.6 grams.

39. Pyragaryite, a rose-colored mineral.

40. The Nova Colônia do Sacramento was the southernmost outpost of Portuguese America, located in modern Uruguay. Antonil here is discussing a throwing weapon consisting of three balls made of this stone, tied together with leather strips, called a *bola* or *bolas*.

41. *Magistral* is a combination of iron oxide and copper sulfate.

42. An *almude* is 4.4 gallons, or 16.81 liters.

The Fourth Part:
The Development and Wealth of Brazil by the Abundance of Cattle,
Leatherworking, and Other Royal Contracts Remaining in This Colony

1. Jacobinas is a city approximately 120 miles from Salvador in the interior of the state of Bahia.

2. The essential thick leather foundation for shoes and boots.

GLOSSARY

Archaic Measurements of Weight, Volume, and Length

almude: 4.4 gallons, or 16.81 liters

arroba: about 32 pounds, or 14.5 kilos

braça: 7 feet 2 inches, or 2.2 meters

legoa: league, distance between 2.7 and 3.8 miles, or 5.5 and 6 kilometers

libra: 16 ounces, or 453 grams

oitava: one-eighth of an ounce, or 3.5 grams

onça: eight *oitavas,* 1.01 ounces, or 28.68 grams

quintal: four *arrobas,* 128 pounds, or 58 kilos

palma: span, a length of about 8 inches, or 20 centimeters

vara: about 43 inches, or 1.09 meters

People and Things

apicus: sand on the beach between high and low tide, used for pottery

areiscas: one of the three types of soil mentioned by Antonil. It is a sandy soil, mixed with clay and not suitable for growing sugarcane.

banqueiro: sugar master's main assistant, a sugar master in training

batido: second-quality sugar

cabucho: sugar at the bottom of the mold

cachaça, claros, and *grapa:* liquid by-products at various stages of the sugar-making process; distilled alcoholic beverages

calcalha: slave women working at the skimming kettle

caldo: one of the terms for liquid sugar as it is being processed

caliz: channel that conducts water to the top of the waterwheel

calumbá: channel cleaner

desmonte: gravel and sand fused together

Emboabas: newly arrived people in the gold mining areas, called this by the *Paulistas,* who discovered the gold

engenho: a sugar mill, used in this text to mean a royal or large mill with a water-powered wheel

engenhocas: smaller sugar mills, as contrasted with royal mills, which are larger

gatos: part of the support for the rollers in the mill

giro: wooden platform for drying clay

guindadeira: female slave who hoists the kettle at the rollers

lei wood: type of strong hardwood used for construction of the mill

macho: first-quality sugar

magistral: a combination of iron oxide and copper sulfate

massapé: the best quality soil for growing sugar cane, good rich earth. It holds moisture well and is normally black.

mel, melado, meladura, and *remel:* names for various stages of the liquid form of sugar—*caldo*—as it is being processed

mascavado: brown sugar

mesas: part of the support for the rollers in the mill

moleque de assentar: pounding tool used in the crating of sugar, also called a "judge"

mourão: a hingelike support on the emergency stop

mulatto/mulatta: a man or woman of mixed European and African ancestry

negro/negras: male or female blacks, when used in this work, slaves

netas: last and smallest of the impurities removed from the sugar

ordenação/ordenações: law/printed collection of laws

pardo: person of mixed race, often European and Amerindian

Paulista: someone from São Paulo

peças: term used by Antonil for black slaves

pejador: emergency water diverter to stop or regulate the turning of the water wheel

porca: the hole in the beam that holds the main axle of the center roller in the mill

rapadura: candy made from liquid cane

Recôncavo: the great bay of Bahia

rodeira: barge used to carry sugar cane or firewood

saloens: red clay soil good for growing some food crops but not good for sugarcane

tarefa: daily allotted task for a slave; a task of cane was 350 bundles of twelve stalks of cut cane, or 4,200 stalks of cane; a *tarefa* was also thirty square *braças* of land, or 4,352 square meters (this equals slightly more than 1 acre)

tarefa redonda: 25 to 30 cartloads of sugar, the amount a mill could press in twenty-four hours

transfogueiros: great iron rods used in tending the fire

venda: four or five molds for liquid sugar, normally filled at the same time

Money and Taxes

consulado: a tax on goods

conto: one thousand, normally used for money, as in one thousand *milréis* (1,000$000)

cruzado: a gold or silver coin, worth 400 *réis* (old *cruzado*) or 480 *réis* (new *cruzado*)

maioria: a tax

milréis: one thousand *réis*, written 1$000

pataca: 320 *réis* ($320)

quindena: a fifteenth

quinto: a fifth, the royal tax on precious metals

réis: the monetary unit used in Brazil and Portugal

tostão: 100 *réis* ($100)

vintena: a twentieth

vintém: small coin worth twenty *réis* ($020)

INDEX

Angola, 39, 113, 140, 208

ambergris, 129, 133

animals: and gold mining, 173, 182; on a plantation, 53, 84, 86, 118–119

apicus (used for clay), 54, 99

arrobas: of gold, 150–151, 154, 158–159, 207–208; of sugar, 50, 81, 86, 93, 98, 104–105, 107–108, 110, 115–117; of tobacco, 123, 130, 136–138

ash: and silver mining, 190; in sugar production, 33–34, 61, 76, 78–79, 84, 119

ash pan, 36, 99

Bahia, bay of (*Recôncovo*): cattle trade and, 197, 199–202, 204–208; city of, 9; gold and, 149, 153, 155, 158–159, 181–182; missionaries, 47; and sugar mills, 9, 15, 18, 55, 58, 60, 63, 76–77, 95, 104, 114, 117; taxes paid in, 50, 107

bananas, 85, 93, 107

basins, 16, 89–90, 119. *See also* cauldrons; kettles; pans

beans, 44, 85, 173, 175

Boa Vista, mountains of, 173–174

cabucho (sugar at bottom of the mold), 104, 109

cachaça, 84, 86–87, 103. See also *claros; rum*

Cachoeira, 123, 132, 136–137, 177, 181, 216n1

Caeté, 146, 149, 172

caldo, 69–71, 77–78, 80–82, 84–88, 90. See also *mel*; *melado*; *meladura*

carpenters, 15–17, 39, 73–74, 141. *See also* tools

carts: used for firewood, 77; used for sugar cane, 15–16, 30–31, 53–54, 60, 62, 70, 73, 110, 118, 202; used for tobacco, 130, 136

Cataguás, mines of, 146, 150, 172, 176

cattle, 62, 125, 156, 159; cows, 156, 205; herds of, 202–203; prices, 204–205; ranches, 197–201

cauldrons, 16, 31, 33–34, 63–64, 70–71, 76–78, 80–88, 90–91, 99, 119. *See also* basins; kettles; pans

chickens, 47. *See also* animals

children, 18, 20, 43–44, 56, 58, 90, 112, 118, 127, 130–131, 152

churches, 16, 19, 26–28, 41, 44, 135, 192, 209–210

claros (drink made from sugar cane), 34, 85, 90

clergy, 27, 41, 47, 134–135, 152, 192

copper, 16, 49, 78, 80–81, 85–86, 88, 91, 100–101, 112, 113

Curitiba, 146–147, 200

customs house and taxes: on gold, 153–154, 179; on leather, 206, 208; on sugar, 51, 115–116, 120; on tobacco, 130, 136–137, 140. See also *quinto*

Espirito Santo, 148, 199

firewood, used in sugar production, 16, 19, 30–31, 41, 49, 54, 63, 74, 76–78, 100, 202

fish, 47, 140, 145, 175

flour: from corn, 156; wheat, 190. *See also* manioc

forests, 16, 19, 31, 39, 54, 75. *See also*
hardwoods, firewood

goats, 53, 58–59, 84, 156. *See also*
animals
God, 5, 22, 24–28, 41–42, 44, 47–48,
58, 193, 210; taxes paid to, 37, 107,
136, 209
gold: damage to economy caused
by, 192–193; as decoration, 42, 157;
exports of, 207–208; finding and
extracting, 183–186; general mines,
147–148, 155; karats, 150–151, 158;
miners, 152–155; mines, 112, 145–146,
154, 191; as money, 40, 155–157, 208;
obligation to pay royal tax on, 161–
171; prices paid for, 158–159; qualities of, 150–151; in Rio das Velhas,
149; in rivers, 175, 179, 186; routes
from São Paulo, 172–175; routes
from Rio de Janeiro, 176–179;
routes from Bahia, 181–182; taxes
on, 153. *See also* mines
government officials, 140, 154, 171,
192, 209
Grande River, 175, 199
guests, 16, 18, 47–48, 54

hardwoods, 73, 78
Heaven, 5, 23, 210
Hell, 40, 76
horses, 9, 17, 30, 42, 45–46, 49, 54, 58,
155, 157, 204; mares, 53

inns, 16, 47, 155, 160

Jacobinas, 197, 199, 204–205, 218n1
judges, 44, 152, 167, 179
justice, 22, 34, 108, 153, 165, 167–169,
171, 192

kettles, 16, 34, 70–71, 76–78, 80–87,
93–94, 99–101, 103, 119. *See also*
basins; cauldrons; pans
knives, 98, 105, 119

laborers: free, 48, 134; slave, 41, 61,
100, 106, 129, 134
ladles, 82, 84–85, 88–90, 100–101
land: selection of for planting sugar
cane, 53–58; on a sugar plantation,
17–19, 31, 43, 51, 61; tenants and, 15,
20–22, 24, 37, 107; for tobacco, 125,
130, 132
law, 19, 40–41, 44, 51, 140, 152; relating to King's right to *quinto*,
161–171
lawsuits, 19, 21, 23–24
lawyers, 21, 37, 46, 51, 153
Lisbon, 115, 123, 136–138, 206

manioc (cassava): flour, 42, 140, 156;
growers, 202; leaves, 126; planting
of, 16, 31, 41, 44, 53
mel, 36, 85–91, 95, 99, 101, 103, 107,
109, 133. See also *caldo; melado;
meladura*
melado, 78, 80–81, 85–86, 88–89,
90–91. See also *caldo; mel; meladura*
meladura, 82, 85–87, 90. See also *caldo;
mel; melado*
merchants: and cattle, 203, 204; and
sugar, 17, 27, 46, 49–51, 110, 112, 120;
and tobacco, 148, 155, 159
mills: building housing, 63–69, 95;
firewood on, 76–79; first day starting, 28–34; furnaces on, 76–79;
lands of, 37, 53–54; merchants and,
49–51, 193; name of, 9; out of operation, 27, 91; overseer, 30–34;
people needed in, 70–72; processed
sugar, 38; resources need for, 15–17,

30, 112; royal and others, 9, 76, 94; slaves and, 39–44, 91, 99, 157; tenants and, 22–24, 51, 107; water on, 20, 31. *See also* plantation; planter; slaves

money: alms, 47; cattle drive and, 204; for chaplains, 25; for children, 45–46; for firewood, 16; for lawyers, 20; loans, 17, 27, 49–51; for pottery workshop, 100; profits made in selling to miners, 160; spent on parties, 44, 49; stealing, 171; sugar and, 112; tobacco and, 138. *See also* gold; *oitavas;* prices

Mortes River, 148, 175, 179

nails, 16, 67, 97–98, 108, 115

native peoples, 5, 145, 147–148, 152, 154, 159, 188, 204

oitavas: and gold panning, 150, 186; and gold prices, 147, 158–159; and *libras* of gold, 146; and the mint, 151, 208; payment for gold share, 154; prices of goods in mining areas, 155–157. *See also* gold; money; prices

Olinda, 197, 199

Ouro Preto, 147–148, 150, 159, 172, 175, 179–180

oxen: as used on sugar plantations, 9, 15–17, 19, 23, 30, 45–46, 49, 53–54, 58–59, 61–62, 75, 84, 110–111; in gold mining, 156, 202, 205. *See also* cattle

pans: and gold mining, 150, 183–184, 186; and sugar production, 33, 78, 80–84, 86–91, 119. *See also* basins; cauldrons; kettles

Paraíba River, 149, 199

Pernambuco: cattle in, 197, 199, 201–202, 205–206; silver in, 145; sugar plantations in, 76, 107, 114–115, 117; taxes from, 207; tobacco grown in, 132, 137; wood from, 207

pigs, 47, 53, 58–59, 84, 119, 173. *See also* animals

plantation: cane on, 60–62; carts on, 62; cattle and, 197, 202–203; household, 45–48; name on crates of sugar, 97–98, 110; needs of, 19, 25, 54; numbers in various areas, 114, 199; overseer on, 16; pottery workshop on, 99–100; production lines of copper vessels on, 80–83; slaves on, 15–16, 39–44; types of land on, 54; types of wood used on, 73–75. *See also* mills; planter; slaves

planter: bookkeeper and, 37–38; chaplain and, 25–28; determining cane to be cut, 61; family, 45–46; guests visiting, 47–48; and his land, 19–21; merchants and, 49–51, 110; needs of, 16, 100; as nobility, 15, 17; overseer and, 29; slaves, 15, 39–44, 71, 100; sugar master and, 33–34; tenants and, 15–16, 22–24, 97, 107; wealth of, 15. *See also* mills

Porto Seguro, 74, 149

ports, 209; and cattle, 208; and firewood, 16; and gold, 152, 157, 160; and sugar, 111, 120; and tobacco, 141

Portugal: Brazilian imports in, 54, 110, 113, 155–156, 158; gold sent to, 193; laws of, 161–171; leather sent to, 202, 206, sugar sent to, 50, 105, 111, 114; tobacco sent to, 123–124, 140–141; sugar planters and nobility in, 15; value of all Brazilian imports to, 207–208; value of Brazil to, 209–210 pottery, 54, 99–100; molds, 93–94. See also *apicus*

prices of: canoes, 75; cattle, 204–205; firewood, 77; food on routes to mines, 173; gold, 158–160; goods, 50, 193; goods in mining areas, 155–157; land, 19; shares in a gold mine, 154; a slave woman, 192; sugar, 15, 50, 111–113; sugar molds, 93; timber, 73–74; tobacco, 123. *See also* money; *oitavas*

Purgatory, 26, 40, 76, 119

quinto: duty to pay king, 161–171; tax on gold, 151, 153, 208; tax of sugar, 107

Recife, 199–200

Rio de Janeiro: and cattle, 199, 200, 202, 205–208; and gold routes, 149, 147, 152–153, 174, 176–182; and sugar production, 76, 114–115, 117, 136

rivers: and cattle, 197–205; and gold mining, 147–150, 159, 183–186; and routes to gold mining areas, 173–179, 181–182

rum, 36, 44, 101, 103, 109, 111, 156, 159. See also *cachaça*; *claros*

Sabarabuçu, mines of, 145, 149, 185

sailors, 39, 77, 111, 134

salaries: of bookkeeper, 37–38; of carpenter, 74; of chaplain, 28; of royal officials at mint, 171; of soldiers, 209; of sugar master, 34, 81; of sugar refiner, 36, 97; of various employees, 49. *See also* money; prices

São Francisco River, 146, 181–182, 197, 199–200

São Paulo, 145–146, 149, 153, 158–159, 172–175, 182–183, 200, 207

Sergipe do Conde mill, 9, 63, 77, 95, 110

sheep, 53–54, 84. *See also* animals

shellfish, 47, 54, 100

shipping, 37, 50, 105, 114, 116, 133, 137, 202

ships, 111–112, 130, 140–141, 155; barges, 60, 62, 74

silver: mines, 145–146, 187–188; refining, 189–191; royal fifth collected from, 161–170

skimmers, 39, 82–84, 87–88, 119, 189

slaves: on boats, 62; and cattle ranching, 204; children of, 44, *claros* and *garapa* distributed among, 34, 85, 90; cost of, 112–113, 157, 159, 192–193; death of, 17, 19; female, 48, 71, 85, 97, 104, 129, 160, 193; food of, 99–101, 202; in gold mines, 159; marriage of, 40; newly arrived, 42, 61; numbers needed to run a sugar mill, 9, 15–17; overseer and punishment of, 29–30, 42–43, 76; *peças*, 16, 100, 212n3; pottery workshop and, 97, 100; quarters, 16; relations with planter, 39–44; religious practices of, 40–41; taxes on, 208; and tobacco cultivation, 131, 152; trade in, 159; treatment of, 17–18, 25, 39–44; work producing sugar, 30–31, 34, 39, 58–61, 70, 75–76, 80–82, 94, 99, 104–107; yaws and, 76

spatulas, 82–83, 89–90, 98, 119

sugar: and cattle, 197, 199, 202; crates produced annually, 114, 207; crating, 22, 37, 62, 74, 97–98, 104–108; faces, 104–105; impounded by creditors, 37; loaves, 16, 95–98, 104–105; making, 23, 63–69, 76–79, 80–84, 86–87, 89–90, 105; master, 9, 33–35, 48, 70, 85, 88–89; mill, 9, 15, 18;

molds, 37, 93–94, 99–103; names
of, 90, 105; planter, 15, 17, 19–21, 23,
27; prices of, 112–113, 115–117, 156;
refiner, 30; refining, 54, 93; selling,
49–51; types of, 101–104, 109–111;
weighing, 107–108
sugar cane: cooking process (liquid),
33–34, 63–69, 84–86, 90, 94; cutting, 60–62; droughts, 17, 58; fields,
9, 16, 31; fires, 31; milling, 28, 60;
milling in rollers, 30–31, 33, 69,
70–72; planting, 53–54, 58; qualities
of, 33, 49, 56, 81, 102; rainfall and,
58, 118; stalks of, 83, 89, 93; *tarefa*,
31, 41, 57, 60, 70; transport, 30–31,
62, 74, 77, 91, 99; from tenants,
15–16, 20, 22–23, 30, 49, 51, 60, 107;
weeding, 55–58

tarefa: of firewood, 77; of sugar cane,
20, 23, 31, 57, 85, 91, 213n9; *redonda*,
70
thieves, 26, 58, 140, 171
tiles, roofing, 49, 63, 86, 95, 100, 190
tenants, 16, 33, 45, 193, 202, 209,
212n1; relations with planter, 15, 17,
19, 20, 22–24, 25, 39, 49, 97, 107
tobacco, 112, 123–124, 138–139, 193,
202, 209; cost in Minas, 156; cost
of one roll, 137; curing, 129; ground
and sifted, 133; harvesting, 127;
medicinal benefits of, 134–135;
planting, 125–126; rolling, 130–131;
second and third harvesting, 132;
smuggling, 140–141; taxes on, 136;
value of total annual production,
207
tools: used by carpenters, 16; used
in sugar making, 34, 80, 82–83,
88–89, 95, 97, 98–99, 108. *See also*
carpenters

vagrants, 48, 192
Velhas River, 146, 149–151, 155, 172,
175–176, 180–182, 186, 197, 201

water, 56, 96; and cattle, 197, 204; for
animals on plantation, 19; and gold
mining, 147, 183–185, 188; power
for mill, 9, 31, 53, 62–69, 93, 106;
for production of sugar, 34, 78, 82,
84–85, 90–91, 99, 101–103; and silver mining, 188–190; and tobacco,
133, 141; wheel, 70, 73
weights, 98, 107–108
whales, 129, 133, 207
women: and gold mining, 152, 193;
and sugar production, 29, 31–32,
39, 42, 84, 91, 97, 104; and tobacco
production, 130
woods. *See* forests

Library of Congress Cataloging-in-Publication Data
Antonil, André João, 1650–1716.
[Cultura e opulência do Brasil. English]
Brazil at the dawn of the eighteenth century / André João Antonil; translated
and edited by Timothy J. Coates, completing a partial translation begun by
Charles R. Boxer; preface by Stuart B. Schwartz. — 1st ed.
p. cm. — (Classic histories from the Portuguese-speaking world in translation; 1)
ISBN 978-1-933227-44-3 (pbk.: alk. paper)
1. Brazil — Economic conditions — Early works to 1800. 2. Sugar growing —
Brazil. 3. Tobacco — Brazil. 4. Gold mines and mining — Brazil. I. Coates,
Timothy J., 1952– II. Boxer, C. R. (Charles Ralph), 1904–2000.
III. Schwartz, Stuart B. IV. Title. V. Series: Classic histories from
the Portuguese-speaking world in translation; 1.
HC187.A613 2012
330.981'032 — dc23 2012022043